The DISCERNING PARENT'S GUIDE TO TODDLER BEHAVIOR:

From Power Struggles to Connection

The DISCERNING PARENT'S GUIDE TO TODDLER BEHAVIOR:

From Power Struggles to Connection

VICTORIA C. ANG-NOLASCO, MD
Foreword by Queena N. Lee-Chua, PhD

Copyright – © 2023 Victoria Ang-Nolasco, MD

All Rights Reserved. This book or any portion thereof may not be reproduced or used in any manner whatsoever without the express written permission of the publisher except for the use of brief quotations in a book review. For permission requests, contact hello@discerningparenting.com.

Note to Reader: The content provided here is for educational purposes and does not take the place of professional advice. Every effort has been made to ensure that the content is accurate and helpful for readers at publishing time. However, this is not an exhaustive treatment of the subject. No liability is assumed for losses or damages due to the information provided. You are responsible for your own choices, actions, and results.

This book is not a substitute for consulting a professional, or for getting intervention if recommended. Reading this book does not create a doctor-patient relationship with the author.

Where applicable, names and identifying details have been changed to protect privacy. In the interest of brevity and to better illustrate some concepts, at times multiple stories have been combined into one narrative.

Publisher:
Hatch and Grow, Inc.
G/F Total Mabini Office Building corner Mabini-San Sebastian Street
Barangay 33, Bacolod City, Philippines
hatchandgrow.org

ISBN: Paperback: 978-1-64775-767-0

Editor: CSusanNunn.com
Cover Art: Genevieve Yap, MD
Typesetting & E-book: Amit Dey | amitdey2528@gmail.com
Cover Layout: Angie of @pro_ebookcovers

**Go to
discerningparenting.com/behavior
and get the free companion guide and bonus material.**

DEDICATION

For the parent who has been criticized over their child's behavior – This book is for you.

EDITOR'S NOTE

There are so many schools of thought on disciplining our children, where is one to turn?

As we unfold into the years 2023 and beyond, we must give credence to all the research that is happening daily and moving us forward in the world. Among that research is child development and discipline. How things were done in the past is not always the way forward.

All the research, such as on the development of a child's brain, has brought us to a deeper understanding of how our children, even when they are toddlers, respond to us. What their capacity is. These things are hugely important.

Even teaching our children to show respect has changed a bit, from "respect your elders" to now teaching our children to show respect for all. But how can we teach them these fundamentals if we don't show them respect? Their response outward to the world will reflect how they have been treated during these formative years and beyond.

It may surprise you, but Positive Parenting came on the scene in the 1920s when Viennese psychiatrists, Alfred Adler and Rudolf Dreikurs introduced Positive Parenting strategies to the United States. Parenting experts and programs across the world have since refined and championed various Positive Parenting[1] Solutions.

---

[1] https://www.ParentingforBrain.com/what-is-positive-parenting/

So, you can call it a modern version of a well-documented way to teach our children about respect, trust, and love from the time they are toddlers. As you read this book, you will be able to understand how the concept of Positive Parenting builds a trusting foundation for both you as the parent(s), and your child. We believe discipline should not be a form of punishment but can be used as a teaching moment. In this book, a short read for busy parents, you will discover the foundation of Positive Parenting, what it really means, and why it works.

C. Susan Nunn,
editor, mom, grandma, and now a great-grandma X2

TABLE OF CONTENTS

Foreword xiii

Introduction xvii

Chapter 1: Power Struggles Decoded: Is Your Child Spoiled or Naughty? 1

Chapter 2: The Key to A Joyful Parenting Journey – Work with The Brain and Not Against It 13

Chapter 3: Understanding Your Child's Behavior 23

Chapter 4: Positive Parenting Strategies to Build a Strong Relationship with Your Child 33

Chapter 5: Positive Parenting Strategies to Handle Behavior Challenges 43

Chapter 6: Common Discipline Challenges. 57

Chapter 7: Screen Time and Behavior 75

Chapter 8: Taking Care of You 97

Chapter 9: When Is It More Than "Just the Terrible Twos"? 105

Chapter 10: Conclusion 121

Breaking the Cycle 125

About the author 129

FOREWORD

Though discipline conjures up "tiger parents" and "terror teachers," it is not a bad word. Discipline simply means instruction, for children to act appropriately toward themselves and others. With self-regulation, children become responsible for themselves, treat others with consideration, and function well in society.

Since discipline is not inborn, children learn from loving role models—parents, and later, teachers and other mentors—and in the process, discipline is eventually imbibed by the self. Thus, discipline is best learned early on. For instance, parents know full well the challenge when they try to impose limits on teenagers who were extremely indulged when they were kids.

But discipline is not punishment, threat, or humiliation. Rather than instilling fear or resentment, positive discipline engenders instead a sense of security in children, who know that their parents care for them enough to expect and model good behavior.

My mentor, National Social Scientist Ma. Lourdes "Honey" Carandang loves to tell this story. When she was working on her thesis decades ago, her toddler son placed a dirty shoe on the table. Honey looked at it and said nothing. Her son then placed another dirty shoe on the table and loudly told her, "Mom, tell me to stop. You should scold me."

Her son instinctively wanted limits, and his mother responded to this need. Honey firmly told him to stop, and he did.

"Discipline is a child's need," says Honey, "and also a child's right. When children are not given limits, many become tyrants. They appear to have freedom, but they feel emotionally insecure." Such insecurity may lead later on to bullying, self-harm, and much more.

Let us discipline with dignity—and this requires balance, which varies with parents and children. While timeout may work for one child, logical consequences may be better for another. But the key is consistency in expectation, presence, love, and care—without resorting to physical, verbal, or emotional punishment that may sometimes veer towards abuse.

Parents often confess that they spank their children if the latter misbehave at home or in school. I gently illustrate with this common example (this example is for kids who are somewhat older than the age group in this book, but it illustrates a similar principle), "If you spank your child, does this pull up their grades? You spank because you are frustrated, which is not the right motive for discipline. Instead of yelling or spanking, go to the root of the problem. Your child cheated because he did not study well. He did not study because he was gaming the whole night. A more effective discipline tactic would be to calmly tell your child that he will only do gaming for 30 minutes on weekends until he exerts more effort in his studies, as evidenced by passing marks on the next test. Also, discuss with your child how you can help him acquire better study habits—when he is in primary school, you can help him go over his studies every day until by middle school, he can already study on his own, with the help of teachers and peers. Tutors are not as effective because they tend to foster dependency—and your child never learns to become an independent learner."

Victoria, of course, is an independent learner, as I witnessed firsthand when she was in my college psychology class years ago. She excelled then, as she excels now. I am proud of how she is juggling motherhood and pediatrics (which includes offering raising-your-children tips, beyond vaccinations and illnesses). She knows full well the struggles faced by parents today, who are caught between the traditional authori**tarian** parenting they themselves experienced (which led many of them to vow to be "friends" with their kids—though being your child's peer group or *"barkada"* is not wise, either) and the permissive parenting on movies, TV, social media these days. Children one up their parents in sitcoms, and fathers are portrayed as particularly clueless—but these depictions are not true to life, either.

Thus, Victoria came up with this helpful book—her second one—to help parents navigate positive discipline with confidence and hope.

Discipline applies to how parents treat themselves as well, which includes rest and recharge. When you are exhausted and irritable, you project these on your children. Not necessarily shopping sprees or massages (though an occasional one is always a treat)—but simple exercise, sound sleep, chats with friends, and what works for me—good books. Start with this one.

Queena N. Lee-Chua, PhD
Mathematics and Psychology Departments,
Ateneo de Manila University

Clinical psychologist Dr. Queena Lee-Chua is one of Asia's foremost authorities on learning and parenting. She is the bestselling author of Learning: What Parents, Students, and Teachers Should Know and 20+ other books – and Mom of economist and author Scott Lee Chua. With her inspiring and transformative talks and classes, she is a beloved and much-sought-after speaker and professor. She has received multiple national awards including The Outstanding Young Filipinos and Ten Outstanding Women in the Nation's Service.

INTRODUCTION

If you look at all the phases describing the early years, especially the toddler stage, one phrase stands out – "power struggle."

You'll never win a power struggle with a toddler. I'm locked in a power struggle with my three-year-old. We hear statements like these all the time.

Before we became parents, most of us had these idyllic images in our heads. The adorable patter of tiny feet. Squishy arms giving endless hugs. Little kids and parents in matchy-matchy costumes posing for greeting cards.

When we saw kids having tantrums in public we thought, "When I have kids, they will *never* act like that. All I need to do is tell my kids that's wrong, so they won't behave that way!"

These thoughts are a far cry from the reality that many of us are facing now.

Your favorite chair has just received a colorful makeover with markers. Your shin is stinging after a kick from a little foot. Or you've said for the 1,432nd time, "It's time for dinner!" but your little one is determined to be chased all over the house.

As a Mom of a three-year-old told me, "When I was earning my master's degree or building my business, I felt I could achieve anything if I put my mind to it. But why doesn't that work when it comes to power struggles with my child?"

I get it. You're smart. You're successful. You're hardworking. You've overcome obstacles and have accomplished difficult projects. You've dealt with tough teachers, intimidating CEOs (or you *are* the intimidating CEO), irate customers, or complaining co-workers – but all of these pale in comparison to facing a screaming toddler.

Now, it's *your* child having tantrums in public. People around you are shaking their heads. And you can imagine them thinking exactly as you did years ago, "My kids will *never* act like that!" Maybe you've even had a well-meaning bystander tell you, "You need to teach your child that it's wrong to behave that way."

With all the parenting books and the wealth of information from the internet and people around us, there's no lack of parenting advice. The problem is – each piece of advice you hear contradicts another!

Family members or friends say you must have strict rules and use strong punishments. But the gentle parents you follow on social media say that your child shouldn't even hear the word "no" at all!

Some people say you need to get angry at your child so they will respect you. They say, "Your child needs to be afraid of you, otherwise they'll never learn to behave well." While others seem to say you should be as unflappable as a Stepford wife and plaster a smile on your face even if your child has been screaming for 20 minutes straight.

That's why I decided to create this book to help you navigate these challenging situations and all of the confusing advice.

When deciding which strategies are correct, it's not simply looking at what's popular, or what someone said worked for them but may or may not be right for you.

Instead, we first look at the results of well-conducted scientific studies. We also look at your situation, in the same way that during medical school, each time we quote a journal, our professors will ask, "How does this apply to your patient?" You also have the values that you hold deeply, and these will also guide you.

The early years are more crucial than many people realize. During this time, kids form their views of themselves, other people, and the world around them. Are they good or bad? Are there people they can trust? Can they succeed, or are they doomed to failure no matter what they do? These beliefs are embedded into kids' brains way before they can logically understand or articulate these ideas.

Handling power struggles in a way that teaches the right skills and values is infinitely easier than correcting problems later when the child is older.

With the principles in this book, it *is* possible for parenting to be a joyful journey.

This doesn't mean your life will always be perfect, like what's portrayed in those laundry soap commercials when we were kids. (Remember the ones where a dancing Mom hugs a smiling child who's wearing a spotless shirt?)

But you *can* break free from power struggles. Unlike a lot of the piecemeal advice we often receive, this book will help you address struggles at the source, instead of feeling like you're constantly fighting fires.

It *is* possible to look forward to each day rather than dreading it, and actually enjoy being a parent. And having a loving and nurturing relationship with your child is not only possible, but it's absolutely essential.

The way to do this is through science-backed Positive Parenting, which will be the focus of this book.

Why Positive Parenting?

If you're reading this, you may fall under one of these three categories:

1. You're convinced that Positive Parenting works, and people around you support your parenting beliefs.
2. You're convinced that Positive Parenting works, but it feels like you're alone in this. It feels like people around you are just waiting for your child to screw up and then they'll shake their heads and say, "See, that's what happens if you don't spank your child!"
3. You're intrigued about Positive Parenting, but you're not sure it even works. You've been hearing all about gentle parenting, but you think, "That's not for me. I'm not patient enough." Or "This works

only for kids who are already well-behaved to begin with. Gentle parenting is only for gentle kids and gentle parents."

A lot of Positive Parenting books focus only on people in the first category. The books say, "Validate and affirm your child's feelings" – and all the adults around validate the child's feelings using well-rehearsed phrases.

But I haven't seen any for those in the second and third categories.

Families where the mere idea of "validate and affirm your child's feelings" is completely alien to them. Then when the Mom is courageous enough to be the first to try it, everyone around says, "That's nonsense! You'll only spoil your child."

The Mom who was raised with spanking, threats, and criticism and knows she doesn't want to raise her child that way. But she gets hardly any support around parenting. Instead, everyone around her says, "We were all raised that way and we turned out fine. Look at how kids today lack discipline."

Couples who are arguing about how to parent their child. One partner says, "Just give in so the crying will stop!" while the other says, "You're being too soft!"

Parents who are trying to practice "gentle parenting" – but they've already been battling with their child for an entire hour just to get their shoes on, until they've lost patience, had a screaming fit, then felt immense guilt about it.

Some people in the Positive Parenting community may not understand struggles like these. A client of mine shares how she joined a paid membership on Positive Parenting that had thousands of members from all over the world.

Once she had the courage to ask, "How can I practice Positive Parenting when the rest of my family doesn't believe in it?" She received a deluge of somewhat disparaging comments like, "This is between you and your child. Why do you care about the rest of your family?" Feeling unheard and intimidated, she deleted her post and then left the group.

The majority of the world's population live in communal cultures where extended family exerts a strong influence on parenting. But most parenting advice assumes that parenting happens in a vacuum, with only parent and child.

If you're the parent of a child age five and under and you resonate with any of these, this book is for you.

In this book, I don't assume that people around you automatically smile and encourage you while your child is screaming or whining. I don't assume that people around you understand that young kids do need to run around and they're not misbehaving when they make a mess.

I understand that your family and the people around you do influence your parenting, and it can take a lot of emotional healing, confidence building, and mindset work to get to the point where you know what you stand for, and you'll stick to it. (I know this not just from the families I work with, but from personal experience too!)

I can fully relate to the struggle of practicing Positive Parenting in a negative world. That's why I start by answering the question – Why Positive Parenting?

At any one time, we're always bombarded with conflicting parenting advice. Here are some examples.

On one hand, we hear:

- "It's bad for your child to hear the word 'no'!"
- "Using timeouts will damage your relationship with your child."
- "You shouldn't teach your child that there's right and wrong. That's just brainwashing."

On the other hand, we hear:

- "Unless you spank your kids, they will grow up to be spoiled and naughty. Kids today are so messed up because we're just not spanking them anymore."
- "Your kids are manipulating you. You need to show them who's boss!"

- "You should teach your child to obey without question otherwise they'll be in trouble."

For each of these conflicting statements, there will always be stories to back them up. "I was raised that way and I turned out fine." "That's what I did with my kids and look how great they are now!"

The human brain is wired to believe stories like these. This is built into our natural reactions from prehistoric times. "Smithson saw a lion in that cave! Avoid that cave!" was useful during prehistoric times, but unfortunately today, this instinct to take stories as gospel truth can get in the way of making good decisions. Because whatever statement you put out, you'll always be able to find stories to back them up.

That's why we want to look at proof. And this means REAL proof – not the "It worked for me therefore it should work for everyone else" kind of proof.

By this, we mean actual research evidence. And what does the evidence say?

There's an entire body of research evidence on the four major parenting styles.

Parenting Styles

These four parenting styles are defined according to two characteristics: *responsiveness* and *demandingness*. *Responsiveness* means how much support parents give. *Demandingness* means how much parents exert influence on a child's behavior and have expectations for how kids behave.

Uninvolved Parenting

If a parent is *not responsive and not demanding,* this is classified as an *uninvolved* parenting style.

A few people may believe that "if you leave kids alone and don't mind them, or tell them what to do they'll grow stronger."

Apart from these few people though, most people do recognize that uninvolved parenting is a huge risk factor in child development.

Research shows that outcomes are the worst for this style of parenting. Being uninvolved does *not* build resilience – rather, it is a huge risk factor for mental health and other problems.

Permissive Parenting (The "Doormat")[2]

If a parent is only *responsive* but is *not demanding*, this is classified as a *permissive* parenting style.

A permissive parent would show plenty of affection, be there for the child, and provide for what they believe the child needs. But the child is allowed to do whatever they want, whenever they want.

A permissive parent doesn't set limits or expectations on child behavior, perhaps believing that they're not good for the child. A lot of the parenting advice we get from social media ("Your kids shouldn't hear the word 'no'") would fall under permissive parenting.

*Authori**tarian** Parenting (The "Dictator")*

If a parent is only *demanding* but is *not responsive*, this is classified as authori***tarian*** parenting. An authori**tarian** parent has very strict rules on how kids should behave, and expect kids to do as they're told, when they're told to do it. They believe kids should obey without question, and they support punishments such as spanking.

Surprisingly, even if they seem like opposite parenting styles, research shows that both *permissive* and *authori**tarian*** parenting actually result in similar outcomes! Both parenting styles are associated with an increased

---

[2] These labels are my own to make it more memorable and interesting! They are in no way a judgment on anyone. If these labels offend you or you don't feel they are useful, feel free to ignore them.

risk of mental health problems like anxiety and depression, as well as an increased risk of continued behavior problems.[3]

Pinquart et al (2018) combined the results of 428 studies across different cultures. Results suggest that authori**tative** parenting does result in better outcomes regardless of culture.

*Authori**tative** Parenting (The Discerning Parent)*

The parenting style supported by the research is the *authori**tative*** parenting style. This means that parents are *both demanding and responsive*.

Now, "demanding" doesn't mean that we put pressure on our kids to achieve more and more at earlier and earlier ages. What this means is we have clear and reasonable rules and expectations on how kids should behave. We set limits on what they can and cannot do. These limits and expectations are comforting to kids.

---

[3] There is an entire wealth of research on parenting styles since Diana Baumrind published her work on parenting styles and child development in the 1960s. Some of them are mentioned in this footnote – in particular if they were recent, or if they combined the results of several studies. You can find more references in the bonus material with this book at discerningparenting.com/behavior.

In Katsantonis and Symonds (2023), children age 9 and below raised with a "hostile" parenting style was associated with an increased risk of mental health symptoms. Katsantonis, I., & Symonds, J. (2023). Population heterogeneity in developmental trajectories of internalizing and externalizing mental health symptoms in childhood: Differential effects of parenting styles. *Epidemiology and Psychiatric Sciences*, 32, E16. doi:10.1017/S2045796023000094

Kuppens and Ceulemans (2018) dived deeper into parenting styles. One of the findings was that when ***both parents*** practiced authori**tative** parenting (which was labeled as "congruent positive authori**tative**" in this research), children had significantly lower levels of conduct problems. Kuppens, S., Ceulemans, E. Parenting Styles: A Closer Look at a Well-Known Concept. *J Child Fam Stud* **28**, 168–181 (2019). https://doi.org/10.1007/s10826-018-1242-x

Research on the permissive parenting style include Kılıçkaya S, Uçar N, Denizci Nazlıgül M. A Systematic Review of the Association between Parenting Styles and Narcissism in Young Adults: From Baumrind's Perspective. Psychol Rep. 2023 Apr;126(2):620-640. doi: 10.1177/00332941211041010. Epub 2021 Aug 17. PMID: 34404305. and Barton AL, Hirsch JK. Permissive parenting and mental health in college students: Mediating effects of academic entitlement. J Am Coll Health. 2016;64(1):1-8. doi: 10.1080/07448481.2015.1060597. PMID: 26151561.

But we don't stop there. We also support them so they're able to meet these expectations.

Authori**tative** parents are liberal with their show of affection. They show respect, listen to their kids, and value their kids' opinions even at a young age.

Research shows that children raised with an *authoritative* parenting style are more resilient, do better in school, have better social skills, have better self-esteem, and are more self-reliant.

It's exactly the *authoritative parenting style* that is supported by Positive Parenting.

Here are some examples that help illustrate the differences between authori**tarian**, authori**tative**, and permissive parenting beliefs:

Authoritarian	Permissive	Authoritative
Situation #1: It's mealtime, and the child doesn't eat.		
"Finish your food, or else!" Or "I worked so hard to prepare this meal and now you won't eat it." (Yes, guilt messages are part of authori**tarian** parenting.) Or "There are so many hungry children in the world, and you won't even eat your food! You're so ungrateful!" Or "For every bit of food you don't eat, you'll get a pockmark on your face when you grow up." (Raise your hand if you heard this one as a child!)	"You don't like to eat this? Come on, I'll prepare whatever you like." (And then proceeds to prepare one item after another and offer it to the child, or chases the child around the house with a spoon)	The child would have a routine in place that includes helping with meal preparation and having a say in what's on the table. Parents also model healthy eating. "You can eat the chicken or the vegetables, and if you don't eat, you'll need to wait until snack time." If the problem persists, we'll need to examine further why the child doesn't eat. Very often, parents receive advice that it's just about "setting limits" when there may be an underlying issue. That's why this book also examines possible underlying issues behind what appear to be behavior problems.

Authori**tarian**	Permissive	Authori**tative**
Situation #2: A child hits a sibling while they're playing.		
"You hit your sister. Now I will hit you, so you know what it feels like." (This doesn't work. Young kids follow what we *do*, NOT what we say.) "Go ahead! Hit your sister again and see what I'll do!" (Aside from being a threat - and threats don't work - young kids don't understand sarcasm and can take things literally.)	"Oh honey, you seem upset. Thank you for expressing it. But don't you think it's a good idea to try and stop hitting?" or "Please stop hitting. Here's your iPad. Just stop hitting and you can play all the games you want!"	Beforehand, the child would have been shown appropriate ways of playing with a sibling. The parent will have introduced a phrase like, "touch gently," and showed the child what this means. If the child hits, the parent or caregiver actively but gently and respectfully stops the child from hitting, perhaps by blocking the hand. The parent calmly but firmly says something like, "No hitting. You can touch gently or give a high five instead."
Situation #3: A child refuses to brush their teeth.		
"Brush your teeth or else your teeth will all be rotten." "You do as I say when I say it. And I say, brush your teeth right now!"	The permissive parent or caregiver may not even enforce brushing teeth, and instead give up when the child resists. They may lament to the pediatrician or dentist, "What can I do? My child refuses to brush his teeth!"	The child has a routine in place that includes brushing teeth and receives age-appropriate assistance in completing the task. The child also has age-appropriate autonomy over the situation, which for a toddler may be something like, "Do you want to use the Cars or Mickey Mouse toothpaste when brushing your teeth?"

From these examples, we see that in authori**tative** parenting:

- We start working on the behavior *before* the problem behavior happens. It's not just a matter of how we respond if a child won't do something that's needed, but what we do the rest of the time.
- We say specifically what the child needs to do.
- Kids are given age-appropriate choices, within limits that are acceptable to the parent.

You'll also see that a lot of the advice and criticism we get fall under authori**tarian** or permissive parenting. Here are some examples.

Authori**tarian**	Permissive
You need to spank your child.	Your child shouldn't hear the word "no."
It's impossible to raise a good human being without spanking.	You should never ask your child to do anything that they don't agree with completely.
Your child needs to be afraid of you otherwise they won't listen.	You shouldn't teach your child that there's right and wrong.
Kids should be quiet, stay seated, not make a noise, and not make a mess.	You shouldn't allow your child to have a tantrum otherwise their brain will be permanently damaged. (I saw this on a Facebook ad!)
Kids who misbehave are bad and/or naughty.	It's your job as a parent to make sure your child is happy all the time.
If you hug your child too much, you'll spoil them.	Just let them have whatever they want so they shut up! (Statements said out of anger or irritation can fall under permissive parenting too!)

Just by looking at this table, you can already ease your mind by knowing that a lot of the criticism you receive is not backed by science! Many parents have told me, "Just by hearing this, it feels like a thorn has been pulled from my chest!"

> The truth is, as parents, we're not perfectly consistent all the time. We may alternate between being permissive and authoritarian and authoritative – and even neglectful – at times. What matters is what we're working towards in our parenting.

As you're reading this, maybe you're thinking, "Oh no, I messed up and let my child have free reign of the house yesterday!" or "Oh no, I shouted at my child when he didn't listen to me – did I scar him for life?"

The truth is, as parents, we're not perfectly consistent all the time. We may alternate between being permissive and authoritarian and authoritative – and even neglectful – at times. What matters is what we're working towards in our parenting. And the fact that you're reading this book means you're on the right track!

And, I'm not just saying this. There's research to back this up![4] Evidence-based Positive Parenting programs have been shown to reduce disruptive behavior and emotional problems in children. Parents are also less stressed, less depressed, and less likely to use harsh discipline – and even experience improved partner relationships. These result in better mental wellness for both parents and kids.

The effect is not just on behavior and mental wellness. Just this year, an article was published that did a systematic review and combined the results of the research evidence on Positive Parenting programs. The combined results showed that kids raised with Positive Parenting during the early childhood years have better mental abilities (IQ, cognition, and reasoning skills) and better language skills too. The effect on language is even stronger in research that included younger children.[5]

Simply listing all the research studies can already take up an entire book, so we have made links to references available in your bonus materials. Head over to discerningparenting.com/behavior and access it for free.

---

[4] While anyone can give parenting advice and call it "Positive Parenting," if research evidence is important to you, it's best to look at programs that have been well studied. One of these is the Triple P Positive Parenting program, and you can check out the research here. https://www.triplep.net/glo-en/the-triple-p-system-at-work/evidence-based/key-research-findings/

[5] Prime, H., Andrews, K., Markwell, A. et al. Positive Parenting and Early Childhood Cognition: A Systematic Review and Meta-Analysis of Randomized Controlled Trials. *Clin Child Fam Psychol Rev* **26**, 362–400 (2023). https://doi.org/10.1007/s10567-022-00423-2

CHAPTER 1

POWER STRUGGLES DECODED: IS YOUR CHILD SPOILED OR NAUGHTY?

I was in first grade, surrounded by my classmates.

"Victoria is Sweet!" One classmate said.

"Pretty!" Another chimed in.

"Obedient!" My classmates took turns chiming in.

"Intelligent!"

"Loving!"

"Excellent!"

"Delightful!"

Then they looked at each other, gave secret "inside joke" grins, and repeated the adjectives over and over – in that particular order.

You can tell my classmates were smart because as first graders, they already knew to tease someone by creating an acrostic for SPOILED!

I was often labeled as "spoiled" by many people around me. It didn't help that I was an only child. Every time I had a tantrum or acted sad, I heard, "You have everything you want. You have all your parents' attention. That's why you're spoiled. You're also being ungrateful – your tantrum shows that you don't appreciate all that your parents are doing for you."

I distinctly remember how my parents were constantly told, "You need to discipline her more!"

Fast forward to when I majored in psychology in college and went on to medical school and learned all about the physiology of the brain. Then I went on to specialize in pediatrics, then train further in this fascinating subspecialty called developmental and behavioral pediatrics.

That's when it hit me. Slowly, all the knowledge and professional experience I was getting made me realize that I was not spoiled.

Okay, so I was not as emotionally regulated as my peers. I didn't have the mature decision-making, social, or perspective-taking skills they had. I had difficulty making friends until my high school years, and it was only when I trained in developmental pediatrics that I realized I am what is now called an "impaired interactive perspective taker."

But tantrums *are* part of the early childhood years.

It is *normal* to feel sad at times. (In fact, one of the things we ask in the clinic when we see kids is whether they're able to show emotions that are usually considered "negative," such as sadness, fear, anger, or embarrassment.)[6]

Maybe your child is being labeled as spoiled, just like how I was labeled decades ago.

Maybe, like my parents, you've received criticism about your parenting, and you're being blamed for how your child is behaving.

If that's you, I wrote this book for you and your child.

---

[6] While it is normal to experience the full range of emotions at different times, we do need to seek help if the emotions seem to be severe or are getting in the way of everyday life. The chapter "When Is It More Than Just the Terrible Twos" will have more on this.

I dream of a world where no child will ever be labeled as spoiled, naughty, or ungrateful. But instead, where all children will be understood, and where all parents get the support they need to bring out the best in their kids.

Let's start by decoding power struggles and misbehavior.

Reasons Behind Power Struggles

Reason #1 – Developmentally Appropriate Behavior

A lot of what we call misbehavior, and the resulting power struggle, is actually what positive discipline experts call "innocent behavior."

"Innocent behavior" is any action that for us, may be undesirable, but is appropriate for your child's level of development.

Here are some examples:

- A one-year-old who repeatedly throws toys to the floor is testing out the skill of "object permanence."
- A one- or two-year-old who repeatedly climbs a sofa even if you've told them no a thousand times is showing a normal developmental milestone, "climbs on furniture."
- A toddler who runs around and touches things around them would be filling their need for exploration – which is essential for normal brain development.
- A toddler who has just learned to say "no" will say "no" a lot, not to defy you, but because they're just learning about boundaries and their separate identity from others around them.
- A young child who doesn't want to share is not being selfish. They're just learning about what's theirs and what's not theirs. Before a child can learn to share something, they need to define first what is theirs. (And besides, if someone came up to you and asked to borrow your phone, would you lend it to them automatically? This can be how it feels for a child who's asked to share a toy!)

That's why we can be locked in a power struggle all day if we try to make young kids go against what they are developmentally programmed to do.

But this doesn't mean we're stuck getting frustrated while they treat grandma's pristine couch like it's their play yard. Instead, we can help kids channel these new skills in more appropriate ways – which we'll cover in this book.

Reason #2 – Inappropriate Situation

Often, whether a behavior is "good" or "bad" is not the action itself, but the situation and how we interpret it.

For example, a child who runs and jumps all over grandma's living room may be labeled as "naughty." But running and jumping at the park or playground would be labeled as "good" (and a child may be scolded for simply staying in one spot in these situations).

A child who makes dinosaur noises at a playmate (especially if the playmate laughs and makes these noises back) is "cute" or "funny." But making these dinosaur noises at an elderly relative may be labeled as misbehavior.

This is why many experts don't label behaviors as "good" or "bad." But they may use terms such as "expected" and "not expected."

But this doesn't mean we don't teach and support them in learning more acceptable ways of behaving. This doesn't mean you should allow your child to make Grandma's living room look as if a hurricane went through it. You can set reasonable limits on where a toddler can run and cannot – while supporting them as they try to figure out these boundaries.

Reason #3 – Interpretation and Labeling by People Around Them

When kids "misbehave," many times it's not the behavior itself, but the interpretation and labeling by the people around them that make it "bad" behavior.

For example, I have seen even very young kids being scolded for scattering flour or powder all over the floor, dropping eggs, or mixing up different condiments (salt, pepper, catsup, and anything they can find on a table) and playing with them. These are all things that I've seen young kids do that have gotten them labeled as "naughty" or "out of control" (and have resulted in their parents getting berated by others).

But go do a Google search – you'll see thousands of "toddler learning activities" that involve all of these!

I'll bet for every "misbehavior" that a young child does, you'll be able to find it used as a "learning activity."

Of course, kids eventually need to learn when, where, and how it's appropriate to do these things. Also, it's perfectly okay to decide what sort of play you'll allow. Just because you see Moms on the internet who make their kids scatter buckets of flour all over the floor, this does not mean you're obligated to do the same. But it does mean that if our kids end up doing this, it's not necessarily misbehavior.

Unfortunately, many of our kids can be in a situation where no matter what they do, their actions are labeled in negative ways. I've seen how active and talkative kids are labeled as "disruptive" or "rude." I've also seen how quiet kids who prefer sitting still are labeled as "snobby" or "overprotected."

Try this experiment. During the next hour that you're with your child, try reframing and changing the labels.

For example, instead of labeling a toddler as "stubborn," say they're persistent and determined. Instead of "hyperactive," think of it as being energetic. Instead of "being difficult" or "just wants to give me a hard time," see how their behavioral struggles can be a form of communication. Even "failing" is a part of learning.

I know this can be a struggle, especially since our view of behavior is colored by all that we have experienced since childhood. Or people may look at us like we've sprouted horns the moment we try to reframe kids' behavior in a more positive way! But in this way, we are changing society to be kinder, more understanding, and more inclusive – and ultimately we become advocates for a better future for our kids.

> *It Can Be Cultural*
>
> How our kids' behaviors are labeled and interpreted can depend on our culture too. For example, in some cultures, you're expected to look someone in the eye when you talk, otherwise, it can be seen as a sign of dishonesty. In other cultures, this is expected only from adults. Kids are expected to look down or keep their heads bowed, and a child who looks an adult directly in the eye is considered rude.
>
> In some cultures, it's okay for kids to talk with adults as if they're equals, and for kids to express their opinions freely. In other cultures, kids are expected to speak with adults in a deferential way, and some cultures discourage kids from speaking unless spoken to.
>
> The takeaway from this is that the "correct" behavior can be confusing, and the same behavior can be labeled in different ways depending on the culture and the situation.
>
> Some kids automatically pick this up by imitating people around them. But many kids don't. So, for example, if you want your child to speak with adults in a certain way, you may need to teach this explicitly.
>
> This is especially difficult for kids who had limited contact with the outside world during the years of the pandemic. All they saw was how the people in their own homes behaved. If they didn't get to see how other kids behave around adults and saw only adult-adult interactions, even with you telling them, it will take a lot of practice and conscious effort for them to learn this.

Reason #4 – Developing Skills

For a child to behave well, a lot of factors need to come together.

1. They need to understand what is expected of them. If it's something a parent or another adult tells them to do, they need to understand what is said.

2. They need to understand *how* to do it. For example, if they're told, "Pack away your toys," the child needs to know what to put where.
3. They need the ability to perform the task. If a child is asked to trace worksheets, they need to have the fine motor skills to hold the pencil properly and follow the lines. If a child is asked to stay seated, they need to have the core muscle strength to hold that sitting position.
4. They need an entire slew of what we call *executive function* skills to work together. This means they are able to *stop* themselves from doing competing actions (like running and jumping around when you're telling them to stay seated), *plan* the action, *start* doing it, *switch* from one action to another when needed, and many others!

Adults often label a child "naughty" and say, "They already know what to do. They have done it at some point but they're not doing it now." They will label the child as having motives like, "They're just out to irritate me," or "They just want to win this power struggle."

But if you look at all these things that are needed for a young child to be able to listen, none of these are easy tasks! They need a child's effort and a lot of brain parts to work.

Even for kids who are described as "never listening" or "always in a power struggle," if we track and look at it objectively, we find that the child does listen a lot of the time.

However, the human brain is programmed to focus on the negative. (After all, our ancestors didn't necessarily need to spread the word that a particular tree had delicious fruit, but they did have to spread the word if something was poisonous otherwise the entire clan would get sick!) This is why people often focus on what the child does wrong rather than the times that the child does behave well.

That's why in my coaching programs, I take parents through a 6-step process. This is also the framework guiding this book.

Step 1 – Calibrate

> We calibrate our understanding of a child's behavior. We also calibrate what we expect from our kids *and* ourselves.
>
> In this step, we clearly define the behavior that we would like to improve. It's difficult to simply say, "I want my child to behave." "I don't want my child to be spoiled." Or "I want my child to stop being so naughty."
>
> What exactly do we mean by "behave"? Exactly what is the child doing that leads us to say "spoiled" or "naughty"?
>
> When you plan a trip, do you say, "Oh, I want to go somewhere north"? While some adventurous folk may do that (simply go on a vacation without a clear destination in mind), generally, if you *want* to get somewhere, you need to be clear first on where you are going.
>
> That's why we need to be clear about our expectations and the behaviors we want to see.
>
> Also, don't try to fix everything all at once. This is a recipe for overwhelm! Start bit by bit. This book contains many strategies, but you don't need to do them all at once.
>
> This is also what I follow in this book. We start by understanding our child's behavior before going on to the other steps.

Step 2 – Calm

> We create an environment of calm, so we set up both you and your child for success. Instead of feeling like parenting is a constant struggle, in this step, we work through what we can do to the environment so that it's *easier* for us to remain calm, and it's easier for our kids to behave better.

Step 3 – Care

For your kids to be okay, you need to be okay too! That's why in this book I've included an entire chapter on your wellness as a parent. When I work with my coaching clients in this step, I take them through a meditative journey that helps them work through childhood wounds that may be affecting their parenting.

We don't realize it, but the experiences we had when we were very young (yes, even the ones we don't remember) – all of these influence our default reactions. How we react to stress and our beliefs about ourselves and our loved ones – research shows that all these were formed during the first few years of our lives.

That's why I often find that simply knowing parenting strategies is not enough. I work with clients to "reprogram" these automatic reactions, so we're able to be calmer during stressful times.

Head over to discerningparenting.com/behavior where I have a video that explains all of this.

Step 4 – Connect

Many books about parenting skip this step. They go right to strategies like doing timeouts, or what to say when your child misbehaves. That's why many parents follow these strategies, then get frustrated when they don't work for them!

Often, when I hear "Positive Parenting isn't working for me," I find that the "Positive Parenting" advice they hear misses this step.

Many parenting influencers explain *connection* in this way – Connect first before correcting. For example, if your child kicks you, start by saying, "I know you're feeling upset now and that's why you kicked." But *connection* goes beyond just saying a few "magic connection phrases" when the child is already misbehaving.

Connection is strengthening your *entire* relationship with your child. It really is the foundation of parenting. Research shows that the relationships a child experiences during the early years can impact everything from their long-term success in life to how healthy they are as adults (and even whether they're likely to get heart attacks or autoimmune diseases)! That's why building a strong and secure relationship with your child is essential to their development and well-being.

Step 5 – Communicate and Coach

We often don't realize that kids are expected to follow many unwritten rules at any given time. Often, we take it for granted that kids should know what to do. And when they don't, they're labeled as "misbehaving."

When kids are at the park and they stay beside their parents, they can be labeled as "aloof." One of the Moms I worked with was even told, "You're so selfish and you keep your child beside you all the time, that's why she's just standing there beside you!" At the park, people expect kids to run, play, move around, and be rowdy (but different people have different levels of "rowdy" that's acceptable to them).

But when they're at a relative's house, for example, and they run around, they're told, "Your child is out of control!"

All this is confusing for kids!

It can be challenging for parents to communicate their expectations in a way that matches their child's level of development.

Often, adults don't realize they're sending mixed signals that confuse the kids. And this doesn't make us bad – this makes us human! That's why if we want kids to listen, we need to be able to communicate clearly with them what we expect in a way that matches their level of development.

Step 6 – Correct: Navigating Sticky Parenting Issues

Parenting advice often focuses solely on correcting children's misbehavior and how to use Positive Parenting to get around these meltdowns. Yet so many parents find the advice doesn't work.

To top it all off, there's a lot of confusing advice about this too. "Just ignore it." "Just do timeouts." "Don't do timeouts." "Give consequences." "Consequences damage your relationship with your child." No wonder many parents feel like whatever they do, they're always failing and doing something wrong!

Not to mention the age-old advice that we still hear a lot, especially in countries where spanking is legal and common. Many will openly say, "You need to spank. It's impossible to raise a good human without spanking." If parents choose to raise their children without such punishment, any time their kids misbehave, people around them say, "See, that's what happens to kids who aren't spanked."

This book shows you several strategies that are both respectful *and* science-backed.

This is an overview of the principles underlying this book. We often see YouTube videos or social media posts claiming, "Just do these three things and end tantrums forever!" But looking at this process (and I'm sure you know this too from your own experience!) – there's no easy answer.

This book doesn't insist that there's some magical solution to behavior problems that will work for everyone. Rather, this book shows you the pieces of this intricate puzzle called behavior and gives you a map showing how to put them together in a way that works for you.

Head over to discerningparenting.com/behavior to get the Companion Guide and bonuses that come free with this book. You'll also find links to the podcast episodes where I talk about these steps.

CHAPTER 2

THE KEY TO A JOYFUL PARENTING JOURNEY - WORK WITH THE BRAIN AND NOT AGAINST IT

*I*f we want to break free from constant power struggles towards more joyful parenting, we need to work with the brain, and not against it.

Remember, our kids' brains are still under construction. They don't always work the same way that adult brains do. They don't always follow the same logic that makes sense to us as adults.

Do you want to get into more detail about this, as well as surprisingly simple ways to boost brain development? When you sign up for the FREE companion guide that comes with this book, you also get a video about this. Head over to discerningparenting.com/behavior.

Why Is Parenting Today So Hard?

So many factors in our lives today work against our brains. No wonder over 2/3 of parents feel that parenting is harder today than it was 20 years ago![7]

---

[7] https://www.pewresearch.org/internet/2020/07/28/parents-attitudes-and-experiences-related-to-digital-technology/

While there are so many factors behind this – including the COVID pandemic which experts have called a "worldwide stress test" – here are three factors I'd like to highlight in this chapter.

Increased Parental Stress

Parents are constantly stressed, pressured, and overwhelmed. (In the chapter on screen time, I talk more about how being continuously reachable through our mobile devices increases stress and affects parental mental health.)

I understand what it's like to be so depleted emotionally – like a string wound up so tight – that the moment a child has a tantrum, there's no more "give" and all we can do is snap.

Or how we can be constantly on our feet with the demands of both work and family, often waking at the crack of dawn, never getting even a moment's rest, and even five minutes sitting down feels like a luxury. Then when bedtime comes, it's like the light at the end of a tunnel. Only, we're faced with a toddler who resists bedtime and instead wants us to chase them all over the house. When that happens, we interpret our child's behavior of wanting to connect with us as a "power struggle" – and we snap.

That's why this book devotes an entire chapter to parental wellness. Because we can't help our kids regulate if we are unregulated ourselves. Also, the methods in this book are designed to be less taxing on our mental resources than a lot of the complicated advice we often find on the internet.

Lack of Play and Connection with Nature

Kids today have fewer places where they can play freely. Many kids are raised in cramped environments where they'll break something and be interpreted as "naughty" the moment they run like normal toddlers should.

Calming nature scenes are disappearing and being replaced with "modern" structures with constant noise and air pollution. Not only is this unhealthy, but this also overwhelms the senses and makes it more difficult to regulate emotionally. Just think of how different you feel in the middle of a crowded street, with horns honking all over, compared to a field with greenery or a calm beach.

These calm nature scenes are disappearing, and kids are growing up in these noisy and crowded places. No wonder kids are now said to have a *nature deficit disorder* – and this affects only their learning but also how they can cope with stress and regulate emotionally. [8]

There are also fewer and fewer opportunities for young kids to play. Due to the increasing demands and faster pace of the world today, parents often feel pressured to prepare a child for academics from an early age.

The time that, ideally, should be spent for play and exploration – because that's what young brains need – is now devoted to academic work. Of all the power struggles I see, the most common one is related to introducing academic work that kids are not yet ready for developmentally.

Increased Push Towards Earlier Academic Achievement

"I've tried everything – rewards, threats, consequences, explanations, validating feelings – but my four-year-old still refuses to answer worksheets!"

There's this idea everywhere that we can push babies and young kids to do things at earlier and earlier ages if we only buy the right course or enroll them in the right program. And this is stressing out so many parents. They feel this sense of urgency to get their kids to achieve more and more.

Most likely, since the moment Facebook figured out you were a parent, your Facebook feed has been filled with all sorts of advertisements of programs promising to make your child more advanced.

All the time, I hear parents trying these programs and then they don't work – their toddlers won't even pay attention – and they get frustrated with their child or themselves. They think, "Maybe I didn't try hard enough." Or they even tell themselves, "I'm failing as a parent."

---

[8] https://www.takingcharge.csh.umn.edu/how-does-nature-impact-our-wellbeing

What Can We Do as Parents?

Every time something is stressing us out, we need to ask:

- Is this something my child's brain is wired to do?
- Is it appropriate for my child's level of development?

A LOT of the advice we get doesn't take into account a child's age or developmental level.

There's a time and place for worksheets, but not at this age.

The sad thing is, sometimes we make young kids do these activities, in place of other activities that they need more.

Like, instead of running and playing outside, the child spends so much time sitting and doing worksheets. But to develop well, what does the child's brain need? You guessed it – it's the running and the outdoor play. Not the worksheets.

All this pressure is taking its toll on our kids' behavior and mental health. From an early age, they experience that learning is a constant struggle. No matter how hard they try, they can't measure up to the expectations of people around them. The lack of play and movement is making it more difficult for them to regulate.

This leads to fights, frustration, and even tantrums. Parenting ends up feeling like it's always an uphill struggle, like carrying a huge boulder up a mountain.

But if we work with our kids' brains and respect them where they are now – it will be more like riding a bike on level ground.

We still need to guide the bike, but this time, you don't have gravity working against you. It's no longer a minute-by-minute struggle.

And we can be calmer, happier, and more confident parents while bringing out the best in our kids and helping them achieve their full potential.

Working With the Brain Through Positive Parenting

If you go on Instagram or TikTok, you'll see that many people disagree over what Positive Parenting is. To add to the confusion, there are other terms such as "gentle parenting," "peaceful parenting," and others coined by people in the parenting space.

Positive Parenting is also raising kids based on the belief that *all* children are good and *want* to do the right thing given the right opportunity and resources.

Yes, ALL. Even that toddler who bites and kicks everyone in sight. Or the five-year-old who spent the last couple of hours screaming. They are *all* good.

Positive Parenting believes there is no such thing as a child who is inherently bad and needs to be punished so that they'll get in line and have the "badness" stamped out of them.

This means that if kids misbehave, it's not because they're "out to get you" or "that kid is really naughty." But, because *something* (or several somethings) prevents them from behaving as expected.

Many people think that Positive Parenting is simply about not spanking. Or that it's about saying some magic phrases when a child misbehaves, and the child will magically listen (and then when it doesn't work, they conclude, "Positive Parenting doesn't work")!

But it's much more than that. Positive Parenting is a whole belief system and way of life. It's about what we do *all the time* and not just when our child misbehaves.

This is also why, in this book, I show you the different pieces of the parenting puzzle. I use the principles of Positive Parenting along with an understanding of the different aspects of child development and brain psychology.

A lot of the advice out there will focus on only one aspect of Positive Parenting. Like what to do when your child has a tantrum or when your child won't listen. They only give one piece of the puzzle, and that's why it doesn't work, and parents end up doubting themselves and feeling like they've failed.

But we need to start *way* before the time that a child misbehaves. This book takes you through these steps. So, I recommend you read this book from beginning to end. It might be tempting to skip to, for example, the part on tantrums, or the part on how to do a timeout. But don't. Because unless you've built the right foundation, simply adding on a timeout won't work on its own.

The good news is, science-backed Positive parenting is *easier* to do compared with a lot of the advice out there, as you'll see in this book.

> Want to learn more about the research behind discipline methods such as spanking? Or maybe you need to get through the tough times when people criticize your parenting, saying, "Your child needs a spanking!" Head over to discerningparenting.com/behavior and access the FREE *Companion Guide* and bonus material. You'll get an easy-to-understand review of what the current parenting research says about spanking. You'll also get any updates to the material in this book!

Does Positive Parenting Mean We Don't Discipline?

I've often seen on social media, "You need to use Positive Parenting/gentle parenting instead of discipline." I also often hear parents ask, "Should I discipline my child, or should I use Positive Parenting?"

Many times, discipline is treated like a bad word. In fact, when I told one of my coaches that I plan to write a book about discipline, she told me that I'm going to alienate a lot of people who think that discipline means being cruel to kids.

As you can see, I didn't follow this coach's advice to remove the word "discipline" from my book. That's because this is a huge myth that we need to break if we want to raise kids who grow up to be both happy and responsible adults.

Many people believe discipline is about punishment. But if we look at the root word of discipline, it comes from the Latin *discipulus* which means "pupil." This is the same as the root word of "disciple" – yes, describing the relationship between Jesus and his disciples.

So, discipline is *not* about punishing kids when they do wrong, but about helping them learn the skills and behaviors they will need. That's exactly what Positive Parenting does! This means Positive Parenting *is* the best and most science-backed way to discipline a child.

Should I Get My Child's Permission Before Doing Something That Involves Them?

This is a controversial topic!

On one hand, some people say, "I'm the parent. I know what's best for them, and I should be the one who decides. Why do I need to get my child's permission?" Taken to the extreme, it may happen that the child who is being passed around to be kissed by an entire roomful of relatives, and when the child protests, the relatives just find it cute.

(If your extended family doesn't play a major part in your everyday life as a parent, it may be difficult to imagine this situation. But there may have been situations when your child was expected to act more friendly with a bunch of people than what your child is comfortable with.)

On the other hand, others say, "We always need to get our kids' permission for everything that involves them. Otherwise, it kills their autonomy, and they will grow up with a lack of boundaries and a lack of self-respect."

Taken to the extreme, people who believe this may even get to the point that the child doesn't brush their teeth anymore "because they don't want to." And of course, when the teeth decay, they can't even go to the dentist because what child will say yes when asked, "Do you want your teeth drilled?"

Every parent may be at a different point along this spectrum of opinions. If this is a dilemma for you too, here are some tips that can help you resolve this based on an understanding of child development and Positive Parenting.

Discern Between Negotiables and Non-Negotiables

Ask yourself, "Is it necessary? Why am I asking my child to do this?" With the toothbrushing example, it is necessary and for the child's benefit. So toothbrushing should be a non-negotiable.

But with the example of the child being kissed by a roomful of relatives, is it for the child's benefit? Is it even necessary? There are so many ways to show respect, without invading the child's personal space and without spreading viruses from one person to the other!

Look At the Situation from Your Child's Perspective

Based on this, it will become clear that you need to insist on toothbrushing no matter how much your child protests. At the same time, you acknowledge how it can sometimes be uncomfortable – so you'll talk your child through the situation.

Based on this also, you'll be able to discern that you shouldn't force your child to hug and kiss everyone at a gathering. After all, would you like to be asked to do this if you don't feel like it?

This goes for situations like taking away a toy that belongs to one child and giving it to another without permission, then later calling the first child "selfish" if they protest. By putting ourselves in the child's position, we know that we don't like it either when our things are taken away!

Give Age-Appropriate Choices

Even if you need to insist on something, such as toothbrushing, your child can still have autonomy by choosing what toothbrush or toothpaste to use, for example.

So instead of "asking permission" by saying, "Would you like to brush your teeth?" – a better question to ask may be, "Do you want to use the Cars or the Frozen toothpaste?"

As pediatricians, we're taught to do something similar during examinations. For example, if it's non-negotiable that we examine a child with a stethoscope in the clinic, we get their cooperation. (Different doctors would have different ways of doing this – whether by examining Mom or a stuffed animal first or by making it into a game).

Here are some sample situations where it's probably a good idea to get your child's permission:

1. If your child appears to have a difficult time doing something (for example, putting on a shirt or completing a puzzle), instead of automatically jumping in to help, you may want to ask, "Would you like me to help you with that?"
2. If your child seems upset, instead of jumping in and trying to fix everything, it may help to simply sit quietly with them. You can also ask something like, "Would you like me to sit beside you, or would you like a hug?"
3. Allow age-appropriate independence, such as letting them decide if they want to bring a toy along (and which toys to bring) when going out, instead of you making this decision for them.

Advocate For Your Child's Boundaries

Often, it's not the parents who violate a child's boundaries, but other people. You know your child best, and you also have your own intuition and gut instinct on what's okay and what's already a boundary violation.

Personally, I don't like it when strangers or people I hardly know suddenly whip out their phones and take photos of my child. (Especially if it appears to be just a photo of my child. I have more leeway if their kids are in the photo too.)

I have been told there was nothing I can do, and I'm "mean" or "paranoid." But I chose to take a stand on this unapologetically. I would say firmly, "Please don't take photos of my child, and please delete the photos you've already taken."

There are still many situations when I'd stayed silent and then later wish I'd spoken up, but I'm sharing this hoping it gives us more courage to advocate for our kids.

CHAPTER 3

UNDERSTANDING YOUR CHILD'S BEHAVIOR

*T*he toddler years are a critical time for brain development and Positive Parenting plays a crucial role in nurturing this process. About 90% of the child's brain development occurs from about two to about five years of age. Positive interactions, responsive caregiving, and stimulating environments promote neural connections in the brain, laying the foundation for cognitive, emotional, and social development.[9]

Here, we will have a very quick overview of toddler brain development, and what this means for behavior.

Understanding Your Child's Brain

The development of the human brain has fascinated medical researchers and scientists for centuries. Still, to this day, the ongoing neuroscience research continues to dig deeper into our understanding of this amazing process.[10]

---

[9] https://hwcec.org/brain-development

[10] The more we learn about the brain, the more we see the importance of the relationships that we build with them in early childhood. Early relational health is a huge topic, and there's a growing body of research showing that kids need safe, stable and nurturing relationships for healthy brain development. https://www.aap.org/en/patient-care/early-childhood/early-relational-health/

Our early experiences, those that we will never remember, and through the early developmental stages, are highly important as the brain begins to build on its foundation. For instance, a child's early exposure to language and social interactions is so important.

As each part of the brain develops, it has certain distinguishing jobs. There are parts of the brain that tell us when we need to be afraid of something and to either fight back or escape from it – what we call the "fight or flight" response. There are parts of the brain that help us learn and remember things (and these can be different parts of the brain depending on *how* we learn it and *what* is learned)!

There are parts of the brain that specialize in, for example, feeling different emotions, recognizing faces, or taking on the perspective of someone else. (Research has shown that these parts can actually be impaired in some people.)

Then there's the part of the brain that's been called the "higher brain," the "command center," or the "brakes" – and that's what we call the **prefrontal cortex.**

The prefrontal cortex tells us that even if we feel like escaping from the office and going to the mall instead, we shouldn't because we need to finish our work. It tells us that if we want to have veggies for dinner, we need to go to the grocery store today because we don't have any more veggies after we used up that head of broccoli last night. We use this part of the brain for everything from planning a family vacation to deciding if it's a good idea to tell a friend our exact opinion about what she's wearing.

When these brain areas are formed, the cells there go through a lot of shifts. They grow in number. At birth, babies have 100 billion cells. These cells then form connections – until, by the time a child is three, these 100 billion cells will have around 15,000 connections for *each* cell. That's more than all the computers on the internet, multiplied by all the connections! This means all the power of the entire internet, and everything connected to it pale in comparison to the power of a child's brain.

But amazing as it is, their brain development is not yet complete. Each of these connections needs to be coated with a substance called *myelin*.

Myelin is important because it allows messages to travel faster and it makes parts of the brain work better.[11]

Okay, you're saying, this is all fascinating, but what does this have to do with why my toddler won't pack away his toys when I tell him to? What does this have to do with my toddler's tantrum?

And that's a good question.

These different parts of the brain don't develop all at the same time. For young kids, the parts of the brain responsible for the "fight or flight" response and emotions such as fear are much more well-developed than the "higher brain" which helps us make good decisions.

Different parts of the brain get their myelin at different ages. The prefrontal cortex doesn't get myelinated until… the late 20s! For many years, people believed brain development was more or less complete by age seven, which is why seven is traditionally considered the "age of reason." But today, we know that our brains continue developing into young adulthood.

This means that children aren't simply little adults. They don't use logic and reason the way adults do. They don't have the impulse control that adults do. And it's not just because we haven't *taught* them yet and they haven't had enough life experiences. But there's an actual *physical* difference.

This means that a child who doesn't listen or do what they're told, or a child who has a tantrum, is not "out to get you." This is a manifestation of how their brain is still under construction.

But this doesn't mean we need to wait for a child to turn 30 before we expect them to behave well. In fact, this shows why Positive Parenting is so vital starting from the early years. Because it's during these early years that the brain cells and connections are formed which will influence the rest of the child's life.

---

[11] A classic in brain development is the book "From Neurons to Neighborhoods" by Shonkoff and Philipps. https://pubmed.ncbi.nlm.nih.gov/25077268/

We're learning more and more about early relational health – which is how *relationships* during the early years influence everything from how healthy we are as adults to how likely we are to have depression or anxiety.

When you get the *Companion Guide* that comes with this book, you'll also get a video where I talk more about early relational health and adverse childhood experiences. So be sure to sign up for it at discerningparenting.com/behavior.

During this time when our kids' brains are still forming, this is exactly when they need our support. We are their guide. We help them regulate. While their prefrontal cortex hasn't fully formed yet, we support them.

Here are the takeaways:

1. Your child's brain is still under construction. Don't expect perfection. Don't expect them to be able to think logically the way we do.

2. Even when a child *knows* something, it can still be difficult for them to *behave* in that way. If you've tried playing any sport, you know that knowledge isn't the same as actually *doing* something. You *know* that you're supposed to shoot that ball into the hoop, but that's a completely different thing from actually *getting it in the hoop*. Behaving as expected can be just as challenging for young kids. That's why even if they know what they're supposed to do and you've told them a thousand times already, they still misbehave (and that's assuming they understood it – which we can't assume!)

3. Positive Parenting supports healthy brain development.

The Reasons Behind Common Behavior Challenges

Maybe you're at a toy store, and your child throws a tantrum. She wants one toy, and another, and another. She's asked for 23 different toys and has thrown a tantrum because you won't buy the entire toy store and bring it home. You can feel the stares of those strangers whom you feel have labeled your child as "spoiled."

The phrase "power struggle" is running through your mind. But is it really about your toddler wanting more power? Is it really about your toddler showing she's more powerful than you because she can get you to buy any toy she wants if only she screams long enough?

Instead, take a step back and ask yourself this *one* question that will help you through any toddler behavior challenges.

And the question is this… "Is there a demand that my child is not equipped to handle?"

I like to think about behavior as "supply and demand."

We often don't realize this, but at any one time, there are many demands on your child.

Maybe your child is tired, hungry, or overstimulated.

Maybe there are so many things going on at one time – whether it's a lot of rules to remember or many people talking at once.

Maybe it's a situation that has a lot of expectations that may not be developmentally appropriate for a child at that age.

Or maybe it's a situation that isn't a good fit for the child's temperament. For example, the child is naturally quiet, but the child is being asked to immediately interact with a lot of other people. Or the child is naturally active but has been asked to sit still for a long time.

Or then again, maybe it's all of the above!

At the same time, the child also has their "supply" – their ability to regulate their emotions. Or the presence of loving and comforting adults.

When there's a mismatch between the "supply and the "demand" – that's when we have meltdowns and other behavior challenges.

Take the example of the toy store. Bright lights. Rows and rows of brightly colored toys. Maybe several toys are making different noises all at once or kids are running all over the place too. Maybe other kids are crying. Maybe your kid is already tired from the shopping trip or it's nearing lunchtime.

All of these can be too much for your child to handle at one time – becoming a demand that your child isn't equipped to handle.

So instead of all the advice running through your head – "Should I give in? Should I 'show who's boss?'" If you ask instead, "Is there a demand that my child is not equipped to handle?" and realize all the things that are going on, it will open up other options. Maybe the best thing to do is to leave the toy store and go to a place that's a little less overwhelming.

This explains why different kids can have different reactions to the same situation. For example, at a children's party, some kids can enjoy all the games, while others may cry on Mum's lap.

Even the same child can have a different reaction depending on the situation or the time of day. A child who can behave well when well-rested and beside their parents can become a completely different child when deprived of naptime or when suddenly placed in an unfamiliar environment with new people. (And this doesn't make them bad kids! This is a reaction that's been wired into kids' brains for survival purposes!)

Here's a brief overview of some of these factors. The classification is my own to help us remember them, (and is actually arbitrary and can overlap) but the factors are well established in research.

- High demand
    - A mismatch between temperament and the situation (Example: A child who has a high need for order living in a house where there's no routine, or a child with an active temperament in a situation where they're expected to stay still.)[12]
    - Sensory processing difficulties (Example: Some children may have a lower sensory threshold, meaning stimuli that wouldn't bother most people will bother them. An example would be when a child who has tactile sensitivity has to wear a shirt that's stiff and scratchy. That child may behave better when wearing a different shirt! Others have a higher threshold and need strong input to their sensory systems. These kids may need to move and

---

[12] Check out this excellent resource on temperaments of infants and toddlers at https://www.ecmhc.org/temperament/.

jump around a lot, or they may hit, bump, or hurt others without even realizing it.)[13]
- Expectations that are not appropriate for a child's level of development (Example: A two-year-old who's made to do reading drills and flashcards, or a four-year-old who's made to sit down and write letters of the alphabet. Some kids may be able to do them, but many will need to struggle to keep up with these demands.)
- Many unwritten rules and expectations that adults take for granted, but that kids don't understand and also developmentally can't follow all at once.
- Big feelings that the child hasn't learned to express in more productive ways (As adults, we have these too! Except we have more resources – more "supply" – so they are less likely to erupt, hopefully!)

- Low supply
  - Physical factors such as fatigue, hunger, or illness. I can't count the number of times a child is brought to our clinics because they've had a lot of tantrums recently, and it turns out the child is incubating an infection (maybe an ear infection or they may even have tooth cavities that have been bothering them, but they weren't able to say so and no one realized it). This is not to make you panic that your child may be ill, but just to say that this may be more common than we realize.
  - Undiagnosed developmental or learning difficulties. Many kids brought to our clinics for behavior problems turn out to have speech or developmental delays.
  - Lack of attention from a "safe" person or lack of a safe and nurturing environment.

---

[13] For more on this, check out our course on Sensory Play for Toddlers at discerningparenting.com/sensoryplay.

These are just quick explanations of complex situations. With each of these, there are so many nuances. This is not to have us go around labeling or diagnosing kids. Rather, I included this to show why we need to look at the whole picture if we want to help our kids behave better.

Here are three examples of why we can't focus on only one factor without looking at the big picture.

Example #1 – When it comes to tantrums and misbehavior, many times people simply zero in on only one factor. "The child wants attention!" they label the child as "manipulative" and "attention-seeking."

But it's more than that. Have you noticed that there are times your child can play independently, more than during other times? Because it's *more* than "attention seeking."

Example #2 – Some people focus only on a "behaviorist" perspective. "This behavior was rewarded in the past, so we need to stop rewarding it and give negative consequences instead." But if a child has an undiagnosed developmental delay that's preventing them from fulfilling what's required, or the child simply doesn't understand the unwritten rules of a given situation, rewards and consequences won't be effective.

That's why we need to look at the big picture. The child's developmental level. Physical well-being. Sensory profile. Temperament and personality and how well they match the demands of the situation. Feelings and emotions. The actual situation.

Sometimes, when I tell people about these, they say, "So what should I do? I simply allow my child to misbehave?"

That's not the case! Rather, we start by *understanding* the factors, so we know how to help them.

Some time ago, I remember getting a text message from someone. She said, "My tummy hurts. What medicine should I take?" I told her that I can't simply prescribe something without understanding *why* her tummy hurts.

She went ahead and took some painkillers. The next day, her tummy ache was worse – and she ended up being confined in the hospital for a kidney infection.

I'm sharing this story not to make you worry every time you have a tummy ache. But this shows why we can't simply say things like, "All the child needs is a spanking!" because just as there are so many reasons why someone can have a tummy ache, there are so many factors that influence how a child behaves. I hope this chapter has helped you uncover them. This is one of the first things we do in my parent coaching programs.

CHAPTER 4

POSITIVE PARENTING STRATEGIES TO BUILD A STRONG RELATIONSHIP WITH YOUR CHILD

When we think about building a positive relationship and connecting with our kids, we often think of that weekend getaway or a grand vacation for "family bonding." While these are great, you don't need to wait until some future date before you can connect with your child. Connecting is all about the *small moments in each day* that wire your child's brain for early relational health.

Be Truly Present with Your Child.
Many times, we can be in the same room but not together. Gadgets or other commitments can get in the way of being truly present with the people around us.

That's why being present with our kids can be easier said than done. It can be a challenge because we always want to be "doing" something. We want to be constantly planning the next activities with our kids so that it's rare we get the time to simply enjoy being with them.

I know I'm guilty of this, and I need to remind myself that over and above any planned activities, it is *real* interaction that my child needs most.

Researchers call these *serve and return interactions*. I talk about them all the time because that's how important they are! I like to call them the "parenting magic wands" because they help with everything from learning to behavior to good health – and are extremely easy to do. There's absolutely no preparation, no cost, and no materials involved.

Here's how you do serve and return interactions. Just like a tennis match where one player serves and the other returns, your baby or toddler will give a "serve" by looking, pointing, or trying to get your attention in some way. You "return" by acknowledging the "serve." You name or talk about what your child is looking or pointing at, then pause so your child can respond. This goes back and forth until your child's attention moves on to something else.[14]

So, the next time you're with your child, spend some time just being with them without worrying about any agenda or plan. Instead, give them your full attention and do serve and return interactions.

Listen To Your Child

I know it can be challenging to do this when there are so many things to do and our kids are simply talking about Paw Patrol or Peppa Pig.

Often, kids are told to shut up – and when we take the time to hear their opinions, bystanders sometimes say we're "spoiling" them.

But communication is a habit that's built up over a lifetime. We can't dismiss our kids' ideas today, and then later wonder why, as teenagers, they won't talk to us.

Listening means trying to make sense of what our kids are saying, then helping them identify the thoughts behind them, without judgment. For example, "It sounds like you're excited over what Marshall and Chase did." Or, "You seem upset that the blocks keep falling off your toy truck."

Often, we can be tempted to dismiss what kids are feeling. That's because as parents, we love them so much and we don't want to see them upset! "That's nothing – we'll fix it!" Or "There's nothing to feel sad about!"

---

[14] Check out our YouTube video on serve and return interactions here - https://youtu.be/0zpboc9z5Kc. Learn more about how serve and return interactions shape a child's brain at The Center on the Developing Child at Harvard University's website - https://developingchild.harvard.edu/science/key-concepts/serve-and-return/

But it's important to acknowledge that we do feel different emotions, and one of the ways to help kids process their emotions is by labeling them.

To learn more about this, get my book *Toddler Talking: Boost Your Child's Language and Brain Development in Three Easy Steps*.

Play with Your Child

Kids today don't get enough free play. Play has become planned and structured to the point that we often don't connect anymore. But play is essential for a child's healthy development.[15]

Through play, kids practice and develop the skills they need to behave and regulate better. Here are just some of the important behavior skills they learn:

- Taking turns
- Handling frustration when they don't get their way
- Flexible thinking and different ways of doing something

Play is a great way for kids to move and explore, which is also essential for brain development and for them to be able to regulate.

When I see kids in the clinic and I ask, "How much time does your child spend playing?" often I get the answer – "Oh, he has football classes for an hour outside every Saturday." That's it? One measly hour in the entire week – and it's a structured activity rather than free play. This is nowhere near enough for healthy brain development.

Play in nature is also calming and helps kids with emotional regulation. I suspect that one of the factors leading to the huge epidemic of behavior and mental health problems today is that we simply don't have nature anymore. Many kids grow up cramped in tiny apartments where they can't run around and where you rarely even see the sky and there's hardly any patch of greenery.

---

[15] Yogman et al. The Power of Play: A Pediatric Role in Enhancing Development in Young Children. *Pediatrics* September 2018; 142 (3): e20182058. 10.1542/peds.2018-2058

As much as possible, choose to live in a place where your child can run, play, and move freely, without someone having to warn them every few minutes because they might get hurt or break something.

My book *"Toddler Talking: Boost Your Child's Language and Brain Development in Three Easy Steps"* also talks about play, so if you don't have it yet, be sure to check it out at toddler-talking.com.

Communicate Clearly What Is Needed, In A Way That the Child Responds

I placed this fourth because before this will work, we need to have built up a healthy relationship with them by doing the previous three things. We can't simply spend five minutes with them and then during the five minutes, teach them what our expectations are.

We need to be clear about what behavior we expect from our kids. When I ask, "What do you want your child to do?" often the answer I get is, "I just want my child to behave." But what does "behave" mean?

Or many times they say, "Be a good boy/good girl." But what does it mean specifically to be a "good boy/girl"?

That's why it's important to define exactly what sort of behavior we expect.

Communicate clearly what you expect in an age-appropriate way. Say what your child should do, not just what they shouldn't do. Offer choices – both of which are acceptable to you. Don't state it as a question unless it's really a question.

Does "Reverse Psychology" Work?

"If there's something you *don't* want your child to do, the best way is to tell them that they *should* do it."

I've often heard this cheeky line in Instagram posts. They may be funny and have thousands of likes, but are they true?

The Oxford Dictionary defines "reverse psychology" as "the principle of subtly encouraging a behavior by advocating its opposite."

For example, parents who believe, "My child does the opposite of everything I say!" may tell their kids, "You're *not* allowed to eat these vegetables!" – believing, "This will make them want to eat the vegetables."

There are three problems with this method:

1. There's no evidence that it works.
2. The fundamental belief behind "reverse psychology" is that kids *want* to do the opposite of what they're told. This approach already labels kids as "bad" and "naughty" from the start. If we start with this belief, we won't be able to truly connect with our kids and appreciate their strengths and the efforts they put into trying to behave well. This goes against the fundamental belief of Positive Parenting that kids actually *want* to do what's right if they know how and they're able.
3. It confuses kids. "I don't get it," goes a toddler's brain (although they can't explain it). "Earlier, Mom told me not to eat the vegetables. Then when I ate them, she seemed happy and satisfied. Now, she told me not to spread the paint all over the walls then when I did, she's upset with me."

When "reverse psychology" seems to work, there may be a gap in communicating what it is we want our kids to do. I'm sure you've heard this one before. If I tell you, "Don't think of pink elephants" – what do you think of now?

So instead of simply saying what we don't want kids to do, or resorting to "reverse psychology," it's much better to communicate clearly about what to expect and teach kids the skills so they actually *can* do it. *This* is what research shows to be effective. It's the process we talk about in this book and the process we use when helping parents within our coaching programs.

Notice Your Child When They're Doing It Right

Many parents are afraid of praising their child. They read articles warning against "overpraising." Or they're afraid, "If my child is behaving well and I say something, I might distract them and they'll end up misbehaving!"

Many people I know have told me, "When we were kids, our parents never praised us. They just told us what we need to do to improve. If they didn't say anything, that's when we know we did well."

But if we want our kids to improve their behavior, we need to notice it when they're doing it right.

If you play any sport that involves hitting a target, whether it's shooting a basket or playing darts, will you ever learn if you shoot and then you never actually see whether or not you've hit the target? You won't!

Noticing our kids' positive behavior and giving praise is the equivalent of showing them that they've hit the target.

A few years ago, in a research project, psychologists divided 95 kids (5-6 year olds) into 4 groups, and praised each group in different ways:

Verbal trait – "You are a good drawer!"

Verbal effort – "You did a good job drawing."

Verbal ambiguous – "Yeah!"

Gestural – Thumbs up or high five!

The results? Praising effort ("You worked hard!") was more effective than praising traits ("You're so smart!"). Even a simple "Yeah!" or saying something like "Awesome!" was more effective than praising traits.

But here's something surprising! In this research, it was actually gestures that were most motivating to these young kids![16]

That's especially true with our toddlers. Praise does not have to be complicated. Simple actions like a smile, a hug, or a high five can mean a lot to them.

Remember, if we truly take the time to observe, every child has something worthy of praise. There is always a win to be acknowledged.

---

[16] Morris BJ, Zentall SR. High fives motivate: the effects of gestural and ambiguous verbal praise on motivation. Front Psychol. 2014 Aug 27;5:928. doi: 10.3389/fpsyg.2014.00928. PMID: 25221532; PMCID: PMC4145712.

When praising your child, remember STAR© :

Specific – Label the behavior that your child did. For example, "Thank you for packing away your toys." Instead of, "You're so well-behaved!" or "You're the best and the brightest!—" it would be better to say something like, "I love how you took turns with your sister for the toy" or "I loved how you tried to answer the teacher's question."

Timely – Many times, we notice kids only when there's something wrong. But whatever gets noticed, gets repeated. Young kids also need immediate feedback. So notice what your child did then acknowledge it right away.

Praise **Actions** – Notice the effort, even if it's not perfect. Kids are still learning!

Be **Responsive** – Look your child in the eye. Give a smile or a hug or do a high five.

Model the Behavior You Expect

The single best way kids learn how to behave is to observe people around them. If we want them to speak kindly and say "please" and "thank you," they need to see us speaking in this way. If we want them to learn patience or gratitude, we need to model patience and gratitude as well.

How often have you seen your child copy your exact movements – down to the exact way you flip your hair or the exact tone of voice you use? They won't just copy you, but the people they see around them.

That's why behavior can be a huge challenge for kids. Because often, they see adults breaking the very same rules they're asked to follow.

Set Up Your Child for Success

Have a routine that sets up your child for success. This doesn't mean you can't be flexible. In your resource library, you'll get a guide on how to create a visual routine that your child can understand. Go to discerningparenting.com/behavior.

Their routine should allow a balance of rest and sleep as well as exercise.

Many kids today are sleep-deprived and don't have enough exercise. Screen time is also an issue (we devote an entire chapter on this), because screen time can take away from movement, rest and sleep, active play, and time with nature.

Within your child's routine, involve them in everyday tasks, instead of relegating them to do their "own thing." Involve kids in age-appropriate chores. This gives them a sense of purpose and fulfillment, which improves their behavior.

Today, kids are often relegated to doing their "own thing" – often with a gadget (or parents stress over preparing complicated activities to "entertain" and "keep them busy"). But the *best* kind of learning happens in the course of everyday activities.

Let me tell you a story. Over a hundred years ago, the overcrowded slum area of San Lorenzo, known back then as the "shame of Italy," had a huge problem with children who were called "wild" and "uncivilized." Their parents were working all day, and these kids – as young as 3-6 years old – were getting into all sorts of mischief and even destroying houses!

The city had to do something. They tasked a pediatrician, who was also the chief medical officer, to solve the problem. She set out to create a setting that was *right* for the children's situation.

They didn't create a "proper" school with tables, chairs, and equipment. During that time, these were usually fixed and adult sized. Instead, she used a few small, child-size chairs that were movable.

They couldn't even hire someone with training and experience in education – which turned out to be an asset because they weren't constrained by "how things were done" during that time.

But she noticed that the kids often sat on the floor and didn't want to sit at the tables. So instead of forcing the kids to sit at the tables, she used some low-cost mats using easily available materials, often those found in nature.

She met the students where they were developmentally and created an environment to set them up for success. They could freely explore and move around. She set up a routine that involved learning through play. Instead of insisting that kids do everything in the same way, she allowed individual exploration – but within structure and limits.

The children helped with doing the chores. They helped prepare snacks and clean up. It was considered part of the routine. "Older" kids (the six-year-olds) helped the younger ones (the three-year-olds).

Guess what happened? The kids' behavior completely transformed! They were no longer the "bad kids" that everyone said they were.

And that's the story of Dr. Maria Montessori and how the Montessori method of education started – all because one pediatrician dared to challenge the norm and create a setting that makes it easier for kids to behave well. (The story of how Dr. Maria Montessori set up the Children's House or Casa dei Bambini is a fascinating one, told in her book *The Montessori Method*[17] and others.)

"Montessori" has turned into a marketing phrase where adding the term "Montessori" to any toy automatically triples its price (whether or not the toy was actually suggested by Maria Montessori). "Montessori experts" on the internet will tell you to do everything from complicated activities to worksheets to turning your home into the perfect Pinterest-worthy playroom.

But that's not the heart of the Montessori method. (Maria Montessori never certified any "experts." But since she did not copyright the term, anyone can use it, whether accurately or not.) The Montessori method started with the near-impossible task of fixing disruptive behavior in kids who had very few advantages in a setting that had very limited resources. Over a century later, what we learn from brain science continues to validate Dr. Montessori's theories on how kids learn and develop.

---

[17] https://openlibrary.org/books/OL5920155M/The_Montessori_method.

CHAPTER 5

POSITIVE PARENTING STRATEGIES TO HANDLE BEHAVIOR CHALLENGES

*I*f you skipped directly to this part, go back and read the previous chapters. It won't work if you only do the strategies in this chapter without doing the others.

On the other hand, simply understanding your child's behavior and doing the strategies in the previous chapter can already help! Many of the clients I worked with report seeing changes just by implementing these.

You don't have to implement all these strategies. If you feel that timeouts and behavior charts are completely against your values, you don't need to use them. They are tools that are there for when you need them. And you may find that implemented in the way described here in this book, they are in line with Positive Parenting after all.

Remember That It's Not About You

Don't take it personally. This can be easier said than done. It's difficult not to take it personally if a child is screaming and kicking you. But especially with all that we've learned about the reasons behind kids' behavior from previous chapters, we know it's not about us. It's not because they hate us or they're "out to get us." It's not because they hate whoever is around them at that time.

Before we can help a child, we need to take an objective look at what is happening. This doesn't mean we're bad parents if we get upset, but instead, we recognize too how we're feeling and separate it from what your child is actually doing and what is happening.

For example, if a child acts aggressively during a playdate, it can be tempting to think, "He got mad at his cousin and hurt her while they were playing. I bet he's jealous because I was paying attention to his cousin. Why is he so controlling of what I do?"

Instead, we can look at all the factors that are going on. Maybe it's near your child's naptime, and he's already had a lot of activity. Maybe it's a hot day, and he's feeling uncomfortable.

It's very easy to make assumptions, but if we train ourselves to look and be objective, we can separate the actual actions from the labels that we give them.

Define The Behavior Clearly

Be specific about what it is that you want to improve. Before you can fix something, you need to clearly define the behavior that is bothering you.

Work on one behavior and one part of the routine at a time. Don't try to fix everything all at once.

Observe the behavior without judgment. In Chapter 1, I talked about the Supply and Demand Model of Behavior and how you can ask the question, "Is there a demand that my child isn't able to fulfill with his current resources?"

Observe too whether there are any patterns. Do tantrums happen more often at certain times of the day? (I'll bet these would be near naptimes and bedtimes, or when your child needs to transition from one activity to the other!)

Don't just observe the misbehavior. Observe the wins, too! I can guarantee that even during what you thought was your worst parenting day, there are still more wins than what went wrong.

Using Consequences

A consequence is a result or outcome that follows a specific action or behavior.

There are two types – natural consequences and logical consequences.

Natural Consequences

These are the automatic results that happen with behavior, without anyone needing to do anything.

For example, if a child refuses to wear a coat when it's cold outside, they will feel cold. If it's time to pee but a child insists on skipping it, they may later wet themselves, feeling uncomfortable as a result. These are the natural consequences of their actions.

Logical Consequences

These are consequences that need someone's intervention. For example, if a child uses a toy to hit a playmate, a logical consequence could be that the toy is taken away (the toy goes on "time out") and temporarily, they no longer have that toy to play with.

Many people in the parenting space will say that you should never use logical consequences and that you should stick only to natural consequences. They say that logical consequences are really threats or punishments, which cause trauma and damage the parent-child relationship.

However, it's not practical to rely only on natural consequences. You don't want to wait for a toddler's teeth to be full of cavities, so they experience the "natural consequences" of not brushing. You may need to introduce a logical consequence such as, "You can't go out and play until you've brushed your teeth." (Some experts will say that the feeling of clean vs dirty teeth is enough of a natural consequence. This may be enough for some kids. But our brains can process the same sensations in different ways. So many toddlers may not mind or may not even be able to sense the difference.)

Here's another example. Most parents would not want to use natural consequences to teach a toddler not to wander away in public places.

(I know there are neighborhoods where families feel safe enough to let even young kids wander on their own – unfortunately, this is not the reality in many places.) It makes more sense to use a logical consequence such as, "If you run away from me while we're at the mall, we'll need to go home. We can go back to the mall on another day when you're ready to walk with me."

Of course, we don't advocate simply handing out a consequence without first building a strong connection with your child and without being proactive. In the wandering in public places situation above, for example, it's not enough to simply wait for the child to wander away and then give a consequence. Instead, we would teach and even practice beforehand how the toddler will walk beside the parent and hold the parent's hand if necessary.

Before using consequences, be sure that the demand is an appropriate one. For example, it would not be appropriate to use consequences for a four-year-old who refuses to answer a set of worksheets. Instead, we review whether or not the worksheets are appropriate in the first place.

There *is* a difference between consequences and threats or punishments. These are nuances that often get lost in bite-sized social media posts and 45-second videos.

Here are the differences between consequences and threats or punishments.

Threats are often delivered in the heat of the moment when a parent is trying to control a child's behavior. They are typically presented in an angry tone and are intended to provoke fear or compliance.

Threats are often vague, exaggerated, or unreal.

Here are some examples of threats.

> *If you don't pack away your toys, you won't get to play with them ever again!*
>
> *If you don't take a bath, the monster will get you! Monsters love smelly kids.*
>
> *Just wait until your dad gets home!*

Examples of punishments are shouting at a child, giving a child the "silent treatment" or refusing to talk with them, spanking a child who's hit someone else, making a child kneel on salt or beans, locking a child in a room after they misbehave, breaking a child's favorite toy when they break a household item, or making a child taste soap after they've said something inappropriate.

Reading the previous paragraph, I know many of us will have different reactions. Some will feel triggered by the extreme cruelty of these actions and think, "Only a horrible person will even think of doing any of these!" Others will think, "But my parents did these while I was growing up, and that's how I learned! How else will my child learn to behave?"

I want to break both myths.

First, if at some point you've done (or considered doing) one of these punishments, take heart. This does not make you a bad person. You are here reading this book. This means you recognize that you don't want to raise your kids this way – and that is a huge and important step.

Second, it's *not* true that these are effective in helping kids learn appropriate behavior. In fact, they model the very behavior we want them to stop. That's why this book shows you many other strategies you can use.

So how can we use consequences – NOT threats or punishments – in a way that's positive and trauma-free, and that will be effective in helping kids learn?

First, the consequence needs to be related to the behavior.

If a child uses a toy to hit someone and that toy goes on "time out" for a few minutes, this is related (and is also a precaution to help prevent further injury).

But if a child refuses to eat and their toys are taken away, this is not related.

Second, you need to communicate clearly what you expect the child to do. The consequence must also be something that can be enforced immediately.

For example, show your child different acceptable ways of playing with a toy, so they know they have many choices and ideas. If the child uses it to hit someone, take it away for a few minutes then let them try again.

This is why threats like "the monster will get you" or "the policeman will get you" are not effective. The child soon learns that these are empty threats. It is also these threats that may be traumatic.

If you feel that you're personally unable to follow through with a consequence, it may be better not to mention it at all. For example, some parents in the heat of the moment may shout, "If you don't behave right now, you won't get any iPad time for the rest of the day!" Aside from it not being clear what "behave" actually means, later on, they may feel completely exhausted and end up giving the child the iPad anyway.

This is one of the biggest reasons why many parents say, "I tried Positive Parenting, but it doesn't work!" Because by "Positive Parenting," what they meant was they didn't spank and instead used consequences in a way that's not effective.

If this has happened to you, this is not a judgment of you. After all, you meant well, and it can be difficult to react rationally to a given situation! I know that I fall into this trap myself and I need to remind myself (and I also find myself apologizing to my child afterward).

Third – and this is extremely important – the consequence must be respectful and realistic.

They are not used to induce fear but to foster understanding and learning. That's why a consequence does *not* need to be unpleasant to the child!

One example of a respectful and realistic consequence is that if a child makes a mess, they help clean it up, instead of someone else automatically cleaning it up for them. And because consequences don't need to be unpleasant, this can work even for kids who enjoy cleaning up.

Many people who are against logical consequences say that they are artificial because they need a parent's intervention for them to happen.

But if we think about it, logical consequences are part of life. If a child consistently doesn't submit homework or study in school, the school might give the child a failing grade. At work, if we miss a deadline, a client or a boss may decide to terminate our services.

Have you ever worked with someone who cried foul when you held them accountable for what they promised? Maybe you decided to terminate the services of a provider who failed to deliver work on time, and they're shocked that you're not letting them off the hook "just this once." Could they have been protected from logical consequences while growing up?

In contrast, implementing consequences rather than issuing threats encourages responsibility and promotes problem-solving skills. This is because consequences allow children to understand the link between their actions and the outcomes, helping them make better choices in the future.

Using Behavior Charts

A behavior chart is simply any tool – whether a wall chart or a sheet of paper – that you use to visually track your child's behavior. Typically, a child gets a stamp or a star when they do something that's listed on the chart.

Behavior charts have gotten a bad rap in some parenting circles. From "being like dog training" to "turning kids into reward junkies," some "gurus" say that we should never use behavior charts.

If you are completely against the idea of behavior charts, no rule says you should use them. However, if done right, there's a place for these tools.

Don't you feel good when you tick something off on your planner? I know that if I have a list of things to do and I slowly tick them off one by one, I feel this sense of accomplishment. That's the idea behind a behavior chart if used properly. Even people who make games know this – which is why many games award between one and three stars depending on how you complete a level!

Here are some tips for using behavior charts:

1. Plan for this together with your child. Talk with your child about the behavior that you'll list on the chart.

2. Keep it simple. Many sites on the internet turn behavior charts into a complex production with a lot of tools and things to buy. If your child is the scrapbooking type and enjoys these, go ahead. But if it will just stop you from actually using it, all you really need is a sheet of paper. You don't even need to buy stars or stickers – you can simply draw them with a pen or crayon.

3. Make it age appropriate. For younger kids, a chart with just one action – such as packing away toys or washing hands – is good. Include pictures too, so your child knows exactly what you mean by "packing away toys." The older a child is, the more items you can add to the chart.

4. It's up to you whether you want to have rewards attached to your behavior chart. Many parents find that young kids respond to the visual reminder and the tracking system, rather than the rewards themselves. Some parents like to give a reward, such as a favorite snack, after a certain number of stars. If you will give a reward, discuss this also with your child beforehand. When deciding how many stars, it's helpful to consider what number your child can count to so he can participate in keeping track.

5. If your child does the action that's associated with the behavior chart, give a star immediately and show this to your child. Tell your child too what they did right!

6. You can also use this combined with a routine chart. You'll find a visual routine chart specifically for young kids in your book bonuses at discerningparenting.com/behavior. You can use this as inspiration for your behavior chart.

7. Keep the behavior chart private. This is between you and your child. There's no need to post this on social media or even let others know you're using one. A lot of the criticism against behavior charts is directed against those that are posted on a classroom wall for everyone to see. These public behavior charts are *not* what we're talking about.

Finally, here are two things to remember about behavior charts.

First, behavior charts are meant to be *temporary*. They are tools to remind your child *while they are still learning a behavior*. You'll eventually want to phase them out. For some kids, just a week or two may be all that's needed, while other kids may need more time.

Second – and I say this with ALL the strategies in this section – none of these strategies will work if it's the *only* strategy you use, or if you skip the strategies in the earlier chapters.

This is where a lot of the objections to behavior charts come from. People are afraid that it sounds like dog training and turns kids into reward junkies. But this won't happen if we take the time to truly connect with our kids, no more than ticking things off on our to-do list turns us into dogs or junkies!

Doing Positive Timeouts

Many people in the parenting space say that you shouldn't do timeouts. Usually, the reason they give is that a child who's misbehaving is already upset, and the last thing they need is to be left alone during the times they need our help the most.

I hear that. And that's exactly what we've been saying in this book – a child who's misbehaving is dealing with a situation where the demands exceed their ability to regulate and behave as expected.

That belief is based on a misunderstanding of what time-outs are. In our generation, some of us were punished with "time-outs" which meant being placed all alone in a room – sometimes even places like dark storage rooms – for indefinite amounts of time. This is *not* a time-out.

Have you experienced feeling stressed and overwhelmed? Maybe you were at work or home, and people just kept making demands of you or your time. Have you ever, in these moments, shouted, "Wait! Time-out?"

I know I have!

As adults, we know that we *need* timeouts.

My husband is an avid NBA fan, so I get to watch a lot of their games. During crucial moments in the game, coaches call a "timeout" – then the players regroup and huddle together before they go back to the game with a focused strategy and renewed energy.

THIS is what time-outs are supposed to be. A child's brain is already in high gear from all the stress responses while they're having a tantrum, or while they're hitting or kicking or screaming. Just as we can't expect NBA players to somehow come up with new strategies while the ball is in play, it's unreasonable to expect toddlers to calm down *in the same situation* that triggered these behaviors in the first place.

That's why time-outs are *not* a punishment. They *may* be used as logical consequences, but these are *productive* consequences because, during a time-out, a child is given the space and the opportunity to calm down and self-regulate.

Here are some strategies that can help timeout be more effective for you.

1. Beforehand, choose a safe and calming space that you can use as your timeout spot. This space needs to be well-lit and well-ventilated. Be sure it's not overstimulating, so unlike what some suggest, there's no need to decorate the space with a lot of toys, posters, and other decor. These can be overstimulating instead of calming. You may place comfort objects such as pillows and blankets. You can involve your child in this choice. For younger toddlers, their play yard can be a good option. For older toddlers, a bed or sofa may work better.

2. Discuss this with your child beforehand when everyone is calm. It may help to say something like, "This space is to help you calm down."

3. If your child hits, kicks, or does the specific behavior that you've decided to use a timeout for, tell them to go to timeout or gently guide them to the timeout spot.

4. Timeouts need to be kept short. For young kids, as little as 1-2 minutes can be effective.

5. During this very short time, stay silent instead of speaking with your child. Remember, this is the time and space for your child to calm down.

While a child is in timeout, it can be tempting to give a lecture. "There's no need to have a tantrum, this is such a small thing! Why did you have to go and do that?!" But lectures like these, whether during a time out or even afterward, are not helpful.

Many gentle parenting experts say that you should never do timeouts, and instead talk with your child and validate feelings. "You're upset because your cousin grabbed your toy. I understand that and that's perfectly valid. But instead of kicking him, you can just say, 'Please give me back my toy.'" This is a great thing to do – but *not* in the middle of a tantrum.

When your child is actively having a tantrum, or kicking and screaming, the "higher brain" has stopped working. The fight-or-flight brain has taken over. When your child's brain is in this state, whether you give a lecture or you validate feelings, it's not going to sink in.

So just give your child those few short minutes to calm down. *Then* when your child has calmed down, that's the time to speak with them to validate feelings and process what happened.

If you are really against timeouts, or if there's simply no space in your house where your child can have a timeout (many families we work with live in multigenerational homes with 20+ adults and kids in one house, and there's simply no quiet and calming space) – then you don't have to use this strategy. You have plenty of other strategies you can use.[18]

---

[18] A very interesting research study combined the results of over 3 decades of research on time outs, here are some of the findings: (1) Time outs appear to be most effective in kids age 3-7 years. (2) Time outs are not meant to be used alone, but in combination with other strategies. (3) The reason and the process of the time out need to be communicated clearly. (4) Short time durations are best. (5) Time outs are *not* about placing a child all alone in a room. In the research reviewed, a chair or even a spot on the floor were used. (6) To help a child remain in time out during the short period of time, a *little* gentle physical guidance (such as keeping an arm around the shoulder) may be used. Physical methods such as using a barrier or spanking should *not* be used. Everett, G. E., Hupp, S. D. A., & Olmi, D. J. (2010). Time-out with parents: A descriptive analysis of 30 years of research. *Education & Treatment of Children*, 33(2), 235–259. https://doi.org/10.1353/etc.0.0091

Planned Ignoring

Use this only for minor and nondestructive behaviors that you want to reduce. Examples include thumb sucking or nail biting.

Before using planned ignoring, ask yourself if it's a behavior that you can reasonably ignore even if your child keeps doing it. If you know you can't, it may be better to use another strategy. For example, some parenting experts recommend *planned ignoring* for tantrums or whining – but you'll need to discern whether this is truly right for you (or even which specific whines, for example, can be ignored and which ones you need to listen to).

That's because you'll need to prepare for the extinction burst. This means the behavior gets worse before it gets better. Don't use planned ignoring if you don't think you can handle the extinction burst.

Remember that we ignore the *behavior* and NOT the child. For example, if you want to use *planned ignoring* for nail biting or thumb sucking, when your child does these behaviors, instead of giving a lecture ("You need to stop that! What will other people think?") – just ignore the behavior completely. This is best if combined with the next strategy which is distraction and redirection.

Distraction and Redirection

This is quite effective, especially for younger kids.

In distraction, you encourage them to perform a completely different action.

For example, in the middle of a tantrum, point to something and ask the child, "What's that?" For some kids, it can get the child to stop long enough to shut off the fight or flight reaction.

When used together with planned ignoring, for example, you can distract a child from nail biting by telling them to play with a toy that needs their hands, such as blocks or Play-Doh. Then praise them when they do so.

In redirection, you encourage the same action directed toward an acceptable target. For example, if your toddler is at the throwing stage, give them something they can throw and tell them where they can throw.

This is *not* about getting stressed or constantly entertaining our kids by always having toys or activities to fill every minute of their day. Rather, it's about *showing* them different choices on what behaviors are more acceptable.

Note: These are just quick and simplified explanations of some strategies you can use. Head over to discerningparenting.com to learn more about our coaching programs, where we explore more strategies and dive deeper into discerning which strategies may be best for you. Together, we create a holistic plan to navigate the challenges you're facing.

CHAPTER 6

COMMON DISCIPLINE CHALLENGES

Tantrums

*L*et me tell you about Ria*, the mom of a four-year-old boy. She started working with me because they were dealing with five or more tantrums a day. She said, "There I was, trying to calm down my child, and at the same time being criticized for what I was doing. This is the first time I've felt helpless. Before this, whatever it was – in my master's, in my business – as long as I put my mind to it, I knew I could make it work. But with parenting, we've tried everything and it's not working!"

Each time I run a survey and ask, "What's your biggest parenting challenge? Number one would consistently be – "tantrums."

And no wonder because research shows that between 87-93% of kids have tantrums! (When I saw this statistic, I thought, only that? Isn't it 100%?!)

If your child is at the tantrum stage, know that you are not alone. Researchers have found that 87% of toddlers 1 ½ to 2 years old, and 91% of kids 2 ½-3 years old have tantrums.[19]

---

[19] Sisterhen LL, Wy PAW. Temper Tantrums. [Updated 2023 Feb 4]. In: StatPearls [Internet]. Treasure Island (FL): StatPearls Publishing; 2023 Jan-. Available from: https://www.ncbi.nlm.nih.gov/books/NBK544286/

Tantrums are to emotional regulation as falling is to learning to walk. When your child first learned to walk, did they simply learn to walk and then never fall again? Of course not!

Do you think, "My toddler is so naughty. He already knows how to walk but he still keeps falling." Or do you think, "I'm a failure as a parent because my baby fell again today while learning to walk"? Do strangers around say, "You're spoiling her! Why is she still stumbling when she already knows how to walk?" Of course not! That would be preposterous!

So why do we expect kids to learn to regulate their emotions right away? Why are kids who have tantrums labeled naughty, and their parents criticized for spoiling them?

Instead, what we said in the first chapter about "demand" and "supply" also applies to tantrums.

Before we go on to what we can do, let's start by defining what tantrums are.

If you've seen what a tantrum is (and as a parent, I think you have!), then surely, we know what tantrums are, right? Kicking, screaming, crying so loud you're sure the entire neighborhood can hear it, right?

But it's not that simple.

Let's say three-year-old Jo kicks, screams, and cries during a shopping trip. Is this a tantrum? 99% of people would say yes.

What if Sadie, who's also three, kicks, screams, and cries (does the same things as Jo) after being stung by a bee? Is that a tantrum? I'll bet 99% of people would say that's *not* a tantrum.

This means that whether something is a tantrum depends *not* on the actions of the child but on the surrounding events *and* the interpretations by the observers!

The thing is, at any one time, as we saw in Chapter 1, there are so many factors that influence how a child behaves. For all we know, on that shopping trip, something upset Jo as much as that bee sting upset Sadie.

During the early years, a lot of what we call tantrums may be more accurately called meltdowns. A meltdown is when a child is no longer able to regulate and process the stimuli around them.

Here are five steps I recommend for when your child has a tantrum.

1. Breathe. Stop, take a step back, and take a few breaths. I know you want to jump in and fix things right away. After all, we're super parents and we want to fix things! But taking even just a couple of seconds to do this will make everything we do afterward more effective.

2. Protect. Make sure your child is safe. Remove any objects that can cause injury. Move your child to a safer space if needed. If you do timeouts the way we recommend in Chapter 5, your child's time-out spot is ideal for this. If you see that someone is in danger of getting hurt, you may need to do this step right away. For example, if you see that your child is about to hit someone, try to "catch the hand before it lands."

3. Observe. What is happening? Look at your child and the situation. Ask, "Are there demands going on now that my child isn't equipped to handle?"

4. Assess. Check for the common tantrum triggers – Is your child tired or hungry? Maybe it's been a very hot day and your child hasn't had a drink for some time. Is there a lot of stimulation going on (such as the shopping trip example above)? Chapter 1 has more on these factors.

5. Help. Help your child calm down. Young kids regulate through what we call "co-regulation" – this means that they regulate by "borrowing" the emotional regulation capabilities of a caring and trusted adult. If the environment is overstimulating, this may involve bringing your child to a calmer space.

During a tantrum, this isn't the time to give explanations. "You don't need to be upset that your playmate grabbed your toy. See, you have many more nice toys!"

> Young kids regulate through what we call "co-regulation" – this means that they regulate by "borrowing" the emotional regulation capabilities of a caring and trusted adult.

When a child has "flipped the lid," their brains are not receptive to these explanations.

Try not to assume also what motives a child has. Many people jump to conclusions and assume things like, "Your child is so manipulative!" While it may not be easy – especially if your child has a tantrum in public – don't feel discouraged either. Your child's tantrum does *not* mean you're a bad parent.

What happened with Ria? During our first session, we went over possible causes (which you have in Chapter 1! Do you notice we keep going back to Chapter 1? It's so important!) – and it turned out an untreated chronic ear infection was a contributory factor. "I felt as if a thorn had been pulled out," she recalls. She wasn't being a bad parent.

Over the next few sessions, we went over applying the strategies from the previous chapters to her situation. By the end of our sessions, they were down to less than one tantrum a week, and when the rare tantrums would happen, they wouldn't last beyond a few minutes.

Your book bonuses come with a video that explains these five steps in more detail. So be sure to go to discerningparenting.com/behavior and get access.

Not Listening

"My child won't listen!"

Each time I take a survey, this is one of the top three parenting challenges, along with tantrums and aggressive behavior.

Often, as parents, we find ourselves in situations where we feel our child isn't listening to us.

It can be difficult to understand why. When your child isn't listening, we may hear advice like – "You should train your child to do everything you say, the moment you say it!" "If you don't train your child to do everything you say without question, you'll be breeding disrespect!" Many people believe that a child not listening is the result of a power struggle.

But it's often more than that. Consider this: what we view as a single task is really a series of smaller tasks or behaviors.

For example, taking a bath. What we view as a "simple task" is really a task with many steps!

1. Going to the bathroom.
2. Taking clothes off.
3. Getting into the bath or the shower.
4. Putting on soap.
5. Rinsing off the soap.
6. Toweling dry.

Each of these steps could be a potential stumbling block for your child. Maybe they dislike the sensation of undressing, or perhaps the water temperature isn't to their liking. It could be the soap stinging their eyes, or maybe they're scared of slipping on the wet floor while toweling dry.

When we frame the problem as "my child refuses to take a bath," we risk missing these nuances. By breaking down the task into smaller parts, we can identify the exact step where the resistance occurs and address it directly.

So, what can we do when faced with this situation?

Identify the Problem

Pay close attention to your child's behavior during bath time. Do they resist going into the bathroom, or is it the water they're wary of? Perhaps they don't like the sensation of the soap. Identifying the specific issue can guide your problem-solving efforts.

Communicate

Use clear, specific language so your child understands what you're asking them to do.

- Instead of "Behave," specify what you want: "Please put your toys away."
- Instead of "Don't run," say "Walk, please."

Also, consider whether your instructions match your child's developmental level. Examples of demands that may not be appropriate for age would be a one-year-old "not listening" when asked to stop throwing a toy to the ground (it may be better to direct the child instead to where they can throw); a three-year-old "not listening" when asked to answer worksheets (it may be better to remove the demand altogether); or a four-year-old "not listening" when asked to sit still for 30 minutes without anyone to talk with or an interesting activity to occupy them (it may be better to plan for this situation in advance).

Talk with your child too. Their responses could offer valuable insights. Remember, their reasons might seem trivial to you, but they are very real and significant to them. This can be a challenge for kids who are not yet talking well, so we may need to be sensitive to their nonverbal cues. Even kids who are already talking may still default to simply refusing if they are upset.

Reframe the Task or Problem-Solve Together

Once you've identified the problem, involve your child in finding a solution. This not only makes them feel heard and valued but also more likely to cooperate.

You can also reframe the task to make it more fun. For example, instead of giving an order to "pack away your toys," you can say, "Help the toys go home."

Or try turning the task into a game that will also accomplish the same goal. For example, instead of saying "Wash your hands," you can say "Give this toy a bath" – and your toddler will end up having clean hands too as a result!

Some people would object to using these methods because they feel that it's "coddling" a child. Remember, you won't need to do these forever. What you're doing is framing the task in a developmentally appropriate way.

Reinforce the Positive

Celebrate each step, no matter how small it may seem to you.

To quote Jane Nelsen, author of *Positive Discipline*, "Where did we ever get the crazy idea that to make children do better, first we have to make them feel worse?"

Consider your own experiences. Remember when you were learning a new sport, settling into a new job, or attempting to cook a complex dish for the first time? Did you ace it immediately? Or did you stumble, fumble, and perhaps even make a mess before you eventually got it right? It's in our nature to learn by trial and error. So, why do we sometimes expect our children to be perfect the first time around?

When our kids make mistakes, our instinctive question should not be "What should be the punishment for this?" but rather "How can I help my child learn from this experience and do better next time?"

But here's the tricky part: your child may repeat the mistake. It's easy, then, to fall into thinking, "My teaching isn't working; I must resort to punishment." But hold on! Remember your first few days at that new job or your initial trials with that complex dish? It's important to give our children the same grace we give ourselves when learning something new.

It takes time, patience, and practice to learn and grow. Let's remind ourselves that children are no different. We guide them through their mistakes and support them as they learn to make better choices.

This is the foundation of Positive Parenting – not punishment, but nurturing understanding and growth. And in doing so, we foster a loving relationship that encourages our children to do better, not out of fear of punishment, but out of understanding and a desire to learn and grow.

Remember, when your child seems not to be listening, it's often a sign that they're having trouble with something. By breaking down tasks and addressing each step individually, you can transform these daily struggles into opportunities for understanding, problem-solving, and bonding with your child.

Hitting and Other "Aggressive" Behavior

Hitting, biting, kicking, scratching, or throwing objects are some of the more common behaviors that are labeled as "aggressive." Many people don't realize that a lot of what we label as "toddler aggression" is not deliberate behavior on the part of the child to hurt others.

Many people have different ideas of what is toddler aggression, and whether or not a particular behavior is considered "aggressive." If a toddler hits, kicks, or bites someone else, many people may label this as toddler aggression.

But what about screaming? What about making dinosaur noises, or pointing a toy gun at a playmate? Are these toddler aggression?

How you *perceive* what your toddler is doing may also make a difference in whether or not you label a certain behavior as aggressive. If a toddler trips and ends up kicking someone, most people will not call that aggression.

But what about toddlers who are having a tantrum – and they end up kicking someone? Or a toddler who pushes a playmate while playing?

Many toddlers are still learning to control their bodies. Also, different people process the same stimulus in different ways. What is a playful touch for one person may already be a hard shove for someone else.

What's the takeaway from this? **Toddlers are not deliberately trying to hurt others. It is the interpretations of other people that determine whether an action is considered "aggressive."**

Four (4) Possible Reasons Behind "Toddler Aggression"

1. Difficulty handling frustration and other big emotions

   Toddlers are just getting started on their way to learning to regulate their emotions and actions.[20] The part of their brain called the "frontal cortex," also called the "brakes," won't fully develop until your child is well into their 20s!

   If a child is hitting, biting, or kicking, it may be a sign that they are struggling with emotional regulation or experiencing stress in their environment.

2. Budding skills and independence

---

[20] https://www.zerotothree.org/resources/24-26-months-social-emotional-development

Toddlers are just starting to learn about independence![21] They're also very curious about the world around them. They're like little scientists who test "theories" and see what happens as a result of the actions they take.

In the process of exploring and trying to satisfy their curiosity, they may do things that people interpret as aggression. For example, a toddler may be curious about what happens if he throws a toy to the wall or (oh no!) at your favorite vase.

Toddlers' skills are also growing! They may be feeling the same anger or frustration as a baby who's crying and upset. But now, instead of just being able to express these feelings by crying, they can express them in many more ways – yes, including throwing a toy to the floor in anger.

3. Lack of communication skills

    Young kids are just starting to learn to talk and communicate with others. Even if they already know how to use their words when they are calm, this doesn't mean they have all these skills when they are upset.

4. Presence of trigger factors

    Being tired or hungry, feeling overwhelmed with all that's going on, and being ill are examples of factors that can make it more likely for a toddler to shout, punch, or act in a way that's "aggressive."

What To Do

Understanding the reasons behind toddler aggression does *not* mean we allow them to hit, kick or bite. Sometimes, I see one extreme or the other.

I've seen how some toddlers are allowed to hit and bite others because "they don't understand what they're doing."

---

[21] https://www.cdc.gov/ncbdd/childdevelopment/positiveparenting/toddlers2.html

I've also heard adults say, "I don't care why they're doing it. That's no excuse. We shouldn't try to understand it – we just need to punish the child for it to stop."

But we *can* understand, and at the same time, *take action*.

Follow the same five steps we discussed in the "tantrums" part, but this time, the first action should be "protect." Your biggest priority is to make sure that no one gets hurt, while at the same time showing them that hurting others is not acceptable.

For example, if a child is about to hit a sibling, you can catch their hands before they make contact. You can say, in a firm and matter-of-fact tone, "No hitting."

You may need to remove them from the situation, and if you're doing timeouts, a timeout can give them the few minutes they need to calm down. If they were hitting using a toy, an alternative is placing the toy in timeout.

Yes, you *need* to say that hitting is *not* acceptable. It's not true that our kids should never hear the word "no." BUT we don't stop there. We also need to tell them what to do instead. When they are calmer, remind them, "Touch gently instead." You'll also need to remind them what "touch gently" means.

You may be able to spot the signs that your toddler is about to hit someone, and you'll be able to intervene in time to prevent it. This may be necessary until your child has learned not to hit anymore and can control their emotions and impulses.

Finally, after the child has calmed down, and after you've shown your child what they can do instead, you can let your child try again (such as resume playing with the sibling), even just for a few minutes.

As always, be sure to practice what's in Chapter 4 (including connecting with your child and communicating clearly what you expect) when your child is *not* hitting. These strategies aren't going to work if your child receives attention only when they hit.

Also, be sure to check the chapter, "When Is It More Than Just the Terrible Two's," especially if you feel that the aggression happens frequently or is difficult to manage.

Whining

"I won't I won't I won't I won't I WOOOONNNNN'T!!!!"

"I don't like that! NOOOOOO!!!!"

Whining can test the patience of even the most understanding parents. The drawn-out, high-pitched complaints – shouted at the top of a child's lungs so loudly that you're sure the entire neighborhood can hear it – can feel like an assault not just on your ears but on your parenting.

Take heart that you're not alone in this. Whining is a common behavior in early childhood. It's often a child's way of expressing frustration when they haven't yet developed more effective communication skills.

Here are some strategies to address and reduce whining:

Avoid Escalating the Situation

It's okay to feel upset. There's no need to pretend to be bright and cheery when dealing with whining. This won't be helpful either. After all, how would you feel if you whined to someone, and the person pretended to be bright and cheery?

But escalating your voice or responding harshly can intensify the situation.

Let's say your child refuses the pasta you lovingly prepared over the past two hours and says, "I don't want this!" It can be tempting to get angry and give a lecture about how there are so many hungry children in the world and your child is so spoiled and ungrateful for not appreciating your hard work.

Instead, it's okay to acknowledge that you're upset. But take a breather. Recognize that it's not about you, and often not even about the pasta.

If you've been going through the rest of the book, by now you'll be able to discern the many different factors that go into your child's whining in this situation. Maybe they've had an extra-large snack and are not yet hungry. Maybe their senses are overwhelmed. *None* of them have to do with being spoiled or ungrateful.

Acknowledge Their Feelings

A simple, "I understand you don't feel like eating the pasta right now" or "I can see you're upset because you can't have the toy now" can go a long way in making a child feel heard and understood.

Encourage Proper Communication

Once you've validated their feelings, encourage them to express themselves without whining. This can be done by calmly saying, "I want to help you, but I need you to tell me what's wrong in your normal voice."

Teach Problem-Solving Skills

Use calm moments to teach problem-solving skills. If a child often whines about a specific issue, discuss it during a peaceful time and brainstorm solutions together.

This is one of the things we work on individually with parents in our coaching programs. We identify with them "high-risk" situations when whining, tantrums, or misbehavior are likely. We examine what are the factors, ways to prepare, and what to do – and we rehearse and get everything in place.

If Your Child Asks for Something Without Whining, Reinforce It

Praise your child when they communicate effectively without whining.

Remember, whining is a normal part of a child's development. However, by responding with understanding and teaching more effective communication skills, you can help guide your child towards healthier expressions of their needs and emotions.

Transitions

"It's such a struggle to get my child to stop playing and come down for dinner!"

"How can I get my child to leave the playground without it deteriorating into a tantrum?"

"We're leaving in five minutes!" You tell your toddler, who seems to just ignore it. Before you know it, those five minutes have turned into an extra twenty minutes in the playground, then you're running late.

These questions are very common struggles for parents, and they have one thing in common - they are about what we call transitions. These are the shifts from one activity to another. Transitioning from one activity to another is one of the biggest parenting challenges during the early years.

If you've ever spent twenty minutes convincing your toddler to take a shower ("No mommy, I won't, I won't, I won't take a bath!") – then, later on, struggling nearly as much to get your child to end the shower – you know what I mean. :)

When Sir Isaac Newton said, "A body in motion stays in motion, and a body at rest stays at rest" – maybe he came up with this law while observing toddlers :)

> To make the transition from one activity to another – such as ending playtime at the park and going home or getting dressed – these are just some of the skills that are needed: flexible thinking, planning, self-monitoring, and task initiation. If the child needs to end a particularly engaging activity (such as playing in the park), it also involves impulse control and emotional regulation.

Why Are Transitions So Hard for Toddlers?

That's because **transitions involve several "executive function" skills**. To make the transition from one activity to another – such as ending playtime at the park and going home or getting dressed – these are just some of the skills that are needed: flexible thinking, planning, self-monitoring, and task initiation. If the child needs to end a particularly engaging activity (such as playing in the park), it also involves impulse control and emotional regulation.

Young kids are just starting to develop these executive function skills. Young kids often have more difficulty with transitions than adults do. This is because transitioning from one activity to another requires a lot of resources from their prefrontal cortex, the "higher brain" that hasn't fully matured yet that we talked about in Chapter 1.

To add to this, **most young kids haven't fully developed the concept of time.** They may not yet grasp what "five minutes" or "an hour" means.

Depending on the child's temperament, transitions may be even harder for some. Some kids adjust more easily compared to others (just like how some adults may still have difficulty with transitions).

One of the temperamental traits is adaptability. **Kids with low adaptability may have more difficulty with transitions**. It can feel frustrating to see another child follow immediately when his mom says, "It's time to go" – while your child doesn't do the same. If that's you, take heart – it doesn't mean that your child is "bad" or "disobedient." It just means that your child needs support in handling these situations.

The situation itself can also make transitions easier or more difficult. For example, I notice that when there aren't any other kids around, my son immediately leaves the playground when I say it's time to go. But it can become a struggle when there are other kids his age and he's having a blast with them!

Helping Your Toddler Handle Transitions

Here's what I've found to be helpful.

I'll use the example of when it's time to leave the playground (a situation that was also a big challenge for me!).

BEFORE

Set up your child for success. If you have a choice, go to the playground at a time when your child is well-rested and not hungry. This makes a better play experience too!

Ideally, we'd like to **prepare your child**. "We're only going to the playground for thirty minutes, then we need to go home and have dinner." While your child may not yet grasp the concept of "thirty minutes," talking about your plans will help.

When your child already has the language skills for it, try **giving choices** too. It's important to give them some control over the situation. An example would be questions like, "We only have thirty minutes to go to the playground today. It's your choice – do you want to still go play even if it's just thirty minutes, or do you want to just stay home?" If they choose to still go to the playground, remind them, "If you choose to play, you need to come with me when the time's up."

Prepare your child too for what you'll be doing afterward and help them look forward to the next activity too. "When we come home from the playground, we'll have dinner, and we'll get to talk about the fun things we did!"

A visual routine may also be helpful, like the one included in your book bonuses.

DURING

1. Give a warning. Set a visual or audible timer if needed.

    I give my son a 10-minute warning, then a 5-minute warning. I also show him that I'm setting up an audible alarm on my phone. When the alarm sounds, I say, "Do you hear that? Time's up!"

    If it's ending play time at home, an hourglass timer may also be useful. We also use alarms on Amazon Alexa. My son even sets the alarms himself.

    There may be times when you'll need to leave the playground earlier than planned. Maybe you notice your child seems to be having difficulty with emotional regulation (for example, maybe your child has hit or kicked a playmate).

    You'll need to physically separate your child from the situation, to help your child calm down and regulate. But don't turn this into a punishment. It's not, "You hit your playmate, now you can't play!" Instead, say something like, "Looks like we're not ready to play right now. Let's get some rest, then try again next time." Your child may have a tantrum – but this doesn't mean you did wrong by removing them from the situation.

2. Take advantage of natural transitions.

   It may be easier if there's an external event that can help you make the transition. For example, if one of your child's playmates is leaving too, say, "Oh, looks like Mark is leaving. It's time for us to go too!" Other signs can be things like, "The sun is setting. It's almost dark!"

3. Have a "goodbye ritual."

   Say bye to the playmates. Especially if you have a younger toddler, it may help to say goodbye to the playground, Goodnight Moon style. "Bye-bye slide, we had fun! We're going to have so much fun when we come back here on Saturday!"

4. Give choices. Make it fun!

   Continue giving choices here. Try turning it into a game by asking, "How do you want to go to the car? Do you want to pretend to be a soldier marching towards the car, or do a dinosaur walk?"

Don't forget the other strategies we've been discussing in this book. For example, we can say something like, "We had so much fun playing, didn't we? I know you don't like to go. And I know we'll continue having fun when we sing your favorite songs on the way home."

Look at it from our kids' perspective too. That may be the only time they get to play outdoors or the only time they get to play with other kids.

When I took my certification in developmental play, our instructor said that when she was a child, kids would just leave the house in the morning and play outside all day. They had only one rule – be back when it was dark. I imagine having an arrangement like this would remove so many of the behavior "power struggles" we face today! That's why it's important that our kids get enough time to play outdoors with other kids.

If you feel that your child hasn't had enough play that day, you may need to decide beforehand to allow more time at the playground. It's better to decide on this in advance, rather than to try to enforce a shorter time, only to give in when your child has a tantrum.

You'll also need to communicate clearly what you expect your child to do. Give your child your full attention. Kneel or crouch down so you're at eye level with them. Then take their hand, look them in the eye, smile, and say, "It's time to go!"

Depending on your child's age, you may need to break it down into smaller steps and be more specific.

"Let's say bye to your friends now!"

"Hold my hand."

"Do you want to pretend to be baby duck following mommy duck? I'll be mommy duck. Follow me over there!"

You may need to pause. Sometimes, if you just pause and wait a few seconds, your child will follow on their own.

You may need to repeat. This is especially important for younger toddlers. If your child doesn't seem to be understanding, try repeating the instructions differently. I know a lot of people say that our kids should do what we say, the moment we say it and that we need to say it only once. However, this expectation isn't developmentally appropriate.

Transitions such as leaving the playground, or starting a bedtime routine, may be more difficult if a child is extra tired. You'd think it should be the opposite, right? You'd think that a child who's already tired would be extra willing to leave the playground or go to bed.

But that's not always the case for toddlers! A very tired and sleepy child can still insist on running and jumping around! If you look closely, you'll see the subtle signs that your child is tired already.

AFTER

If all went well, praise your child. "I know it wasn't easy to leave and you still wanted to play. But you came when the time was up!"

If not, plan for next time. Think about what went well, and what could be improved upon. This will help you plan for future transitions. Try asking your child, "What can we do next time so it won't be so hard for you to leave the playground?"

Transitions can be challenging for both children and adults. But with some planning and effort, they can go more smoothly.

If your child has extreme difficulty with transitions and has frequent tantrums with even minor changes in routine, this may also be something to mention to a developmental and behavioral pediatrician or your pediatric care provider.

CHAPTER 7

SCREEN TIME AND BEHAVIOR

*M*eet Lily, the Mom of a lively two-year-old boy named Mio. Mio was born at the height of the COVID pandemic lockdown. Because of this, Lily wasn't able to get help in taking care of him.

Since she works from home part-time, from the time that Mio was six months old, she'd had to keep him occupied with a tablet. Although she'd heard some warnings about screen time, many relatives told her that letting Mio watch educational videos and use educational apps early will make him smarter!

By the time Mio turned one, he was quite familiar with selecting videos on the YouTube app and switching from one app to another. He also started saying words like "bus" and "star" from his favorite nursery rhymes.

When Mio turned two, Lily noted that Mio hardly had any eye contact when others would talk with him. He wouldn't say words like, "Mommy," but he can sing the alphabet song which he often hears from YouTube.

The word he says most frequently is "iPad" – which he often shouts at the top of his lungs from the moment he wakes up.

By the time they consulted me, Lily was teary-eyed, in despair, and feeling extremely guilty. "It's my fault for starting him on gadgets so early. Now he spends nearly all his waking hours on a gadget. From the moment he wakes up, he asks for the iPad. We have two internet connections at home because the moment the internet lags, he throws a tantrum. He has the iPad while he eats, while he brushes his teeth and when we eat out at a restaurant – he has the *iPad the entire day. He pauses a while when the battery runs out, then throws a tantrum again until the iPad is charged enough to turn it on, then he continues watching videos or using apps while it's charging. It's a struggle to get him to stop using the iPad so he can go to sleep.*

Despite the time he spends on the iPad, I'm completely exhausted because it's practically impossible to get him to do anything else. Taking a bath, getting dressed to go outside – he would resist at every step. I don't know what to do. I keep trying to get his interest in playing with Legos or toy cars or drawing or playing with a ball – but he'd play with them for a few minutes then scream for his iPad again. I'm such a horrible parent."

There's one huge question that's all over social media – *Why is parenting today so darn hard?!*

If we browse through social media, a common theme we see is parents complaining about how difficult parenting is. It's on our Facebook feed, in the clinic, or even in casual conversation.

A survey by Pew Research published in 2020 showed that 2/3 of parents say parenting is harder than it was 20 years ago.[22] We wonder why our parents and grandparents managed to raise large families and they didn't even seem as stressed as parents today.

I've even heard some people claim that people today are "weaker." But the world today is simply different. Things seem to be stacked up against parents.

There's the COVID pandemic. Lack of play. Fewer and fewer outdoor spaces. Unrealistic expectations placing extra expectations on both parents and kids. All the misinformation around parenting. ONE huge factor why parenting today is so difficult is screen time.

When I was growing up, no amount of begging could win me an extra episode of my favorite show. (The original He-Man and the Masters of the Universe. Okay, I realize this dates me.) Today, the entire burden of controlling screen time is placed on parents. Our kids can binge-watch

---

[22] https://www.pewresearch.org/internet/2020/07/28/parenting-children-in-the-age-of-screens/

entire seasons of shows in a single day, and it takes Herculean effort to pry them away from the screen.

Maybe you're struggling with a child who's always asking for a gadget and throws tantrums when it's taken away.

Or this isn't a struggle for you, but you're wondering whether screen time really makes a difference in how kids behave.

People have been telling you, "It's no big deal! There's no proof that excess screen time is bad for kids!" Or "This is the age we live in today! The earlier kids are exposed to gadgets, the better they'll adapt to the world and the smarter they'll be."

If you're caught in a screen time dilemma or managing screen time is a struggle for you, know that you're not alone.

It's easy to blame the parents ("Well, then you shouldn't have started giving them a gadget!") but in truth, I believe parents today are being set up to fail when it comes to managing screen time. And I'll tell you why in this chapter – and what we can do about it, so we don't get duped, and we don't get our power and reasoning faculties taken away.

We'll also explore practical tips and strategies to help you monitor and limit screen time while creating a healthy balance.

Many people believe that limiting screen time is just a matter of willpower. But things are stacked against us – and a lot of times simple willpower isn't enough. Our kids today are being raised by screens, and for many, these exert a greater influence on them when it should be the parents who are influencing them. We've talked repeatedly about the importance of early relational health. This gets lost when kids spend too much time on screen media!

A study by the Kaiser Family Foundation showed that kids 8-18 now spend an average of 7.5 hours a day on a screen for entertainment. Over a year, this would amount to 114 days or nearly four months! This has a significant impact on their behavior, development, and overall health. [23]

---

[23] On the average, it's 6 hours a day for kids 8-10 years old, rising to 9 hours a day for kids 11-14 years old and going to 7.5 hours a day for teens age 15-18 years. https://www.cdc.gov/nccdphp/dnpao/multimedia/infographics/getmoving.html

It's not just older kids. According to the 2021 report by the American Academy of Pediatrics, up to 90% of children have used a handheld device by age 1. The majority of children age five and below already have their own internet-connected devices. [24]

In a study of 40,000 children between the ages of 2 and 17, researchers discovered some concerning findings on the mental health effects of screen time and children. Kids who spent more than an hour a day in front of a screen were less curious, less eager to learn about new concepts, and less likely to finish a task.

Additionally, the kids who consumed more screen time had a hard time staying calm when challenged or confronted. They were more likely to argue with their caregivers and displayed lower psychological well-being overall.

The caregivers of the group of 2 to 5-year-olds reported that the children were more easily distracted, more likely to lose their temper, couldn't calm down, and struggled with self-control. These kids had a harder time sitting still, completing simple tasks, avoiding distractions, and displaying perseverance.[25]

Being exposed to screen time at one year of age is associated with an increased risk of developing symptoms of autism spectrum disorder.[26] In one research that involved over 80,000 kids in the Japan Environment and

---

[24] https://www.aap.org/en/patient-care/media-and-children/

[25] Jean M. Twenge, W. Keith Campbell, Associations between screen time and lower psychological well-being among children and adolescents: Evidence from a population-based study, Preventive Medicine Reports,Volume 12,2018,Pages 271-283, ISSN 2211-3355, https://doi.org/10.1016/j.pmedr.2018.10.003.)

[26] Heffler KF, Sienko DM, Subedi K, McCann KA, Bennett DS. Association of Early-Life Social and Digital Media Experiences With Development of Autism Spectrum Disorder-Like Symptoms. JAMA Pediatr. 2020 Jul 1;174(7):690-696. doi: 10.1001/jamapediatrics.2020.0230. PMID: 32310265; PMCID: PMC7171577. and Hermawati D, Rahmadi FA, Sumekar TA, Winarni TI. Early electronic screen exposure and autistic-like symptoms. Intractable Rare Dis Res. 2018 Feb;7(1):69-71. doi: 10.5582/irdr.2018.01007. PMID: 29552452; PMCID: PMC5849631.

Children's Study, in boys, having 1-2 hours of screen time doubled the risk, while those who had 2-4 hours had over three times the risk![27]

Researchers have proposed different reasons why this happens – including missed opportunities to develop the "social brain," such as parts of the brain for processing faces, during a time when it's critical for their development.

Excess screen time affects not just kids, but parents too. Researchers have coined the terms "digitally distracted parenting" and "parental technoference."

Digitally distracted parenting is defined as parental overuse of handheld technology, particularly cell phones, and tablets, in the presence of children. Parental technoference refers to disrupted interactions between a parent and child due to a parent's use of a technological device.

You've probably observed this happening – you're at a restaurant, or on a beach, and you see families who are together, but everyone is on their own gadget, and no one is talking to one another.

In research done by Kaspersky, 82% of parents spend at least 3 hours a day on a mobile device. Around half of all parents and kids spend 3-6 hours a day on a gadget, while over 1/3 of parents spend even more hours than that.[28]

Now, this is just the time that they're *actively* using a gadget.

But what's more revealing is this. At least 45% of parents stay digitally connected throughout the day. This means that even when a parent isn't

---

[27] Kushima M, Kojima R, Shinohara R, et al. Association Between Screen Time Exposure in Children at 1 Year of Age and Autism Spectrum Disorder at 3 Years of Age: The Japan Environment and Children's Study. *JAMA Pediatr.* 2022;176(4):384–391. doi:10.1001/jamapediatrics.2021.5778 Based on the results of this research, among boys, those who had 1 hour to less than 2 hours of screen time had an odds ratio of 2.16, those who had 2 hours to less than 4 hours had an odds ratio of 3.48, and those who had more than 4 hours had an odds ratio of 3.02. The term "odds ratio" is how risk is measured in research like this one, called a "cohort study" where they follow up participants over time. This research did not note differences in girls.

[28] https://www.kaspersky.com/blog/digital-habits-report-2021/

actively using a gadget, they still monitor for alerts and messages at the back of their minds! 65% of parents sometimes skip calls or switch off their devices so they can't be reached, but only 15% do so regularly.

This means that 85% of parents are in what some people now call "continuous partial attention" – they are physically present in the situation, but at the back of their minds, they're checking their phones every few minutes and responding to random notifications that come in.

Because of this "continuous partial attention," there's increased digital stress from being reachable all the time and never being able to take a break. A lot of research has already shown how this digital stress affects mental health.

What Is "Too Much" Screen Time, and Does It Really Affect Kids' Behavior?

Defining "excess" screen time can be tricky since there can be different definitions of what's "excessive."

Most people do recognize that toddlers shouldn't be hooked to a gadget for their entire waking hours. But how about binge-watching an educational YouTube channel for two hours? How about three hours?

Here are the recommendations on the *maximum* amount of screen time by age.[29]

These are all included in the screen time that needs to be limited: watching videos – whether or not they're "educational" (and I have a beef about the top "educational" videos on YouTube Kids – more on that later); using apps – yes, even those educational apps that claim to "teach your child to read"; playing video games; scrolling through social media; watching television.

Here are things that generally aren't included in screen time limits: video chats with other people; making a voice call; listening to music; doing school-related work such as using a word processor (though to be honest, this is a book about kids age five and under – and I hope NO school

---

[29] https://www.healthychildren.org/English/family-life/Media/Pages/healthy-digital-media-use-habits-for-babies-toddlers-preschoolers.aspx

is assigning a child below five any homework that needs to be completed using a computer! Let them develop their hand skills first!)

Having screens continuously on in the background – such as having the television on while no one is watching – and these have detrimental effects too.

If a child is doing online gaming and simultaneously chatting with other players, this IS included in screen time. And besides, online gaming is NOT safe for young kids! It's strange how many people wouldn't allow a child to go to a mall by themselves but think nothing of letting a child loose into the online gaming world.

Screen Time for 18-Months and Younger

For babies as young as 18 months, the recommendation is NO screen time at all. It's okay to do live video chat with family members and friends, though in-person interactions are best.

Screen Time for 18-Months to 2 Years

For young toddlers, continue to limit screen time as much as possible and avoid solo use of media. They are building those movement skills and are busy discovering and interacting with their world. If your very young child watches any TV, choose HIGH-QUALITY educational programming (this does NOT mean searching for "best educational videos for toddlers - more on this later in this chapter).

Watch with them to help them understand (and develop those language and social skills).

Screen Time for 2 through 5 Years

From 2 to 5 years, screen time can be used occasionally, but try to limit your child to an hour or less per day. As much as possible, watch together with your child to ensure that they understand what they're viewing. While you are watching, discuss what they see on the screen and help them apply it to the outside world.

Since the COVID pandemic, many experts say that we can loosen these screen time restrictions. For example, for children who were under lockdown, their only chance to see more of the world may be through watching videos.

I used to agree with this and say that going over the "one-hour limit" may not be a huge deal. But I've personally seen huge differences in behavior and emotional regulation in kids who are "just a little over the limit."

Nick* was a five-year-old boy whose parents described him as having several "rage attacks" a day. For seemingly no reason at all, he would suddenly scream, kick, and punch anyone in the same room. He would also throw toys and other objects across the room.

"I don't know what happened," Nick's mom says. "He used to be such a sweet boy. He was eager, bubbly, and had a twinkle in his eye. He used to love trying different sports for kids and going on playdates. Now he's sullen and withdrawn. All he wants to do is watch videos."

On diving deeper, we found out that Nick was watching videos on either a tablet or television for two to three hours a day. "But we followed – more or less – the screen time guidelines. We didn't let him watch television until he was a year and a half, and we allowed only educational shows."

Increasingly though, it was becoming more and more difficult to control Nick's screen time. What started as thirty minutes a day of "educational" shows gradually became two or three episodes of a child-friendly show.

Then, because of the tantrums and difficulty controlling his behavior – resulting in his parents getting exhausted and needing a break – screen time gradually increased. They also started allowing shows that are rated as "suitable" for kids his age but showed scenes of characters fighting with each other. Even then, they didn't think screen time could be the culprit, since "he's still getting way less screen time compared to other kids his age who are already spending hours playing games on Roblox!"

We initially tried reducing screen time to an hour a day or less, but Nick was still having these "rage attacks." So, I suggested that we do a complete screen fast. I told Nick's parents about how each time we use gadgets, brain chemistry changes in a way that can make it more difficult for him to regulate emotionally. (I explain more about this later in this chapter.)

This was a challenge, as both parents had work that needed to be done online. We also explored different options – including taking a vacation in a remote area that did not have internet access. (I know many families who did this and absolutely loved the experience.)

Here's what they decided. One huge asset they have is their strong relationship with Nick. They talked with him about how they felt the screens were affecting his behavior, and they will try an experiment. For one week, Nick will not be allowed to use any gadgets or screens. His parents also did not use screens while around him.

The first two days were an absolute disaster, so much so that they almost gave up. Nick screamed for the iPad, had more rages than usual, and showed classic signs of going through withdrawal syndrome. While Nick participated in the screen-free activities they'd planned, he kept constantly asking when he can watch again.

They began seeing an improvement by the third day. From several rages a day, he was down to a few short tantrums near bedtime. They felt though that a week of having completely no gadgets may not be enough to "wash away" the altered brain chemistry, so they talked with Nick about extending it for a few more days.

After two weeks of completely no gadgets, they got their son back. He again had that twinkle in his eyes and a spring in his step. He stopped shouting for the tablet the moment he wakes up, and instead takes pleasure in having breakfast with the family as well as enjoying sports and creative activities.

Here's the most important thing – even if they eventually allowed 1-2 episodes of carefully selected shows, they didn't go back to Nick's previous level of screen time, otherwise they may be seeing the same problems again. This doesn't mean things were perfect from then on, but there was a dramatic improvement.

Nick's story is by no means an isolated case. Time and again, I've seen how parents who either drastically reduced or eliminated screen time saw huge improvements in their kids' behavior. And while I've met countless parents who later regret introducing screens early, I've never met a parent who said, "I wish I'd given my child more screen time" or who regrets doing a screen fast.

One of my colleagues did a research comparing two groups of children who were showing symptoms of autism. One group was given the "standard" recommendations which was to limit screen time to an hour or less a day. The other group was told to give zero screen time. Essentially, they were told to do a screen fast.

The results? The group that was given the "standard" recommendation had FIVE times the risk of NOT improving, compared to the "screen fast" group![30]

That's why, although going over the limit once in a while may not have a negative effect on some kids, many kids may be uniquely sensitive to the effect of gadgets on the brain.

So, if you seem to be "stuck" trying different parenting strategies – maybe you've tried every single thing in this book and nothing works, or your child may already be undergoing therapy but it doesn't seem to be working – you may want to consider a "therapeutic trial" of a screen fast. Even if parenting strategies are already working, you may also find that limiting or even eliminating screen time will help them work better.

So how does screen time affect the brain? This is how I think things are stacked against parents and kids today.

Screen time affects both how your child's brain is *built* (and remember, your child's brain is being built right now – as we speak) and how your child's brain *functions*. If you think about a car, it's like screen time affects how pieces of the car are actually being put together – from their sizes to

---

[30] Yatco, Kristyn (2021) Effects of Electronic Screen Removal on Behavior Symptoms Using CARS2-ST and ATEC Among 24-36 Months Old With Autism Spectrum Disorder. Presented at the 4th International Developmental Pediatrics Association Congress

how they are connected, and it also affects things like the fuel, water, and air that are put in.[31]

In addition to these, increased screen time was also associated with an increased risk of language delay, problems with learning math and reading (there goes the argument we often hear that "she learned math and reading early because of screens"), difficulty with fine motor skills that are needed in tasks like handwriting, sleep problems, unhealthy eating, inattention and hyperactivity, conduct problems, and difficulty getting along with others. Kids who received more than the recommended amount were also more likely to either be a bully or be bullied in kindergarten.[32]

These are just the effects of screen time *in general*. Yes, even that nice, animated video of *Old MacDonald Had a Farm*.

The effects are worse if it's *violent* screen time (think – one cartoon character bashing another cartoon character's head). Today, we're so desensitized to violence that almost no one thinks shows like this are violent anymore. Just look at the top shows on YouTube Kids, and you'll see characters hitting each other, darts or objects blasting away, kids getting cheeky with adults – you'll see the exact behaviors that kids are often scolded for if they do these in real life.

---

[31] Hutton, J.S., Dudley, J., DeWitt, T. et al. Associations between digital media use and brain surface structural measures in preschool-aged children. *Sci Rep* 12, 19095 (2022). https://doi.org/10.1038/s41598-022-20922-0 talks about the effect of screen time on how different parts of the brain developed, based on MRI studies. https://hms.harvard.edu/news/screen-time-brain also summarizes the research on the effects of screen time on the brain.

Another research is Hutton JS, Dudley J, Horowitz-Kraus T, DeWitt T, Holland SK. Associations Between Screen-Based Media Use and Brain White Matter Integrity in Preschool-Aged Children. *JAMA Pediatr.* 2020;174 (1):e193869. doi:10.1001/jamapediatrics.2019.3869 and https://edition.cnn.com/2019/11/04/health/screen-time-lower-brain-development-preschoolers-wellness/index.html explains the findings of this research.

[32] Li C, Cheng G, Sha T, Cheng W, Yan Y. The Relationships between Screen Use and Health Indicators among Infants, Toddlers, and Preschoolers: A Meta-Analysis and Systematic Review. Int J Environ Res Public Health. 2020 Oct 7;17(19):7324. doi: 10.3390/ijerph17197324. PMID: 33036443; PMCID: PMC7579161.

Do these really affect kids? You may ask. "I tell my kids that it's just on television, and they shouldn't imitate these." But kids imitate what they see much more than they process what we tell them.

Young kids may not yet be able to learn a foreign language by watching YouTube videos or using an educational app, *but* they can certainly learn to imitate one cartoon character bashing another on the head! So, kids end up *not* learning the things we *think* they're learning on YouTube, but instead learning things we don't want them to.

In the 1960s, Albert Bandura, a psychologist, conducted the famous "Bobo doll experiments." Children in the same nursery class (meaning they were generally of the same age and had the same teacher and exposure in school) were divided into two groups.

One group saw a person behave aggressively towards the doll, while the other group observed a person playing more nicely. Those in the group that saw the person behave aggressively were more likely to also play in more aggressive ways.

But wait, that was in person. Does that apply to violence that kids watch? A few years after, Bandura repeated the experiment but used a video instead of a live person. And yes, the kids who watched the "violent" video did behave more aggressively.

He followed this up with a third part. In this part, he showed two videos – in one video the person was praised for violent behavior, while in the other video, he was punished. Seeing the person being praised for the violent behavior increased the likelihood even further that the child would imitate it.[33]

---

[33] Bandura, A., Ross, D., & Ross, S. A. (1961). Transmission of aggression through imitation of aggressive models. *The Journal of Abnormal and Social Psychology*, 63(3), 575–582. Okay, so sometimes when I cite a research that's decades old, someone will comment and say, "1961! Bah! Why listen to the results of a study that's so outdated?" I have two responses to this. First, this is a study that will likely never be replicated. That's because no ethics board today will approve a research that will deliberately show violent videos to kids. Second, Bandura's research spawned an entire body of succeeding research and influenced what we call social learning theory, which is a continuously growing field. Here is just one of the articles about this. https://hr.berkeley.edu/how-social-learning-theory-works

This is quite scary because today, cartoon characters who act violently are often lauded or rewarded for it – maybe by getting laughs, attention, or simply by being the hero. Our media today doesn't like heroes who are kind and well-mannered. Shows like that are considered "boring," "unrealistic," or as I hear kids say, "cringe." Being "bad" is seen as the new good. Is it any wonder we're facing so many challenging behaviors today?

Even kids as young as four play games where guns are fired, and bombs blow up every few seconds. And then we wonder why there are so many school shootings. And then people say it's because we're not spanking kids anymore. Didn't anyone even stop to think that a contributing factor is how they've been exposed to so much violence, practically from infancy?

Each time I give a talk about screen time, I always explain something called *The Algorithm*.

"The algorithm" is something that's common knowledge in the online world. This means there are extremely sophisticated artificial intelligence programs whose sole job is to keep people hooked. YouTube has an algorithm to make sure you binge-watch. Facebook, Instagram, and TikTok have algorithms to make sure you keep scrolling. Games have algorithms that are designed to keep people playing.

This isn't a conspiracy theory. It's established and standard business practice. After all, these platforms exist to make money. And the longer you stay on the platform, the more chances they have of making money.

When I was learning how to start a YouTube channel, I saw how we can see exactly when people started and stopped watching our videos. A course I took on YouTube said to observe what moments people drop off and to use this knowledge to make future videos more appealing so that people don't stop watching in the middle of a video. There are also similar ways of knowing on a website exactly where users drop off and stop reading.

Now, I can only see data for those who visit my website or Youtube channel. But YouTube, Facebook, Instagram, and other social media platforms see *all* that data about YOU (and about your child or whoever is using the device) across all the platforms they own and wherever their tracking information is included. They know exactly when you start and stop watching, and when you stop the scroll to look more closely at a post.

Over time, they gather more and more data about *you*, so they know exactly what to show you. Most of the time, this can be useful – for example, there was this time I ordered food from a delivery service, then suddenly my Facebook feed was full of delivery services, so I then have several choices. Where it becomes insidious is that this same data is used to keep us scrolling endlessly.

When you see a post, or you get a like, or you complete a level in a game, your brain gets a burst of a brain chemical called *dopamine*. This chemical causes us to feel good. It's released naturally when we get a hug, get some exercise, or do something we enjoy. It shoots up to extremely high levels when doing recreational drugs like cocaine, which is why cocaine is so addictive.

Dopamine also shoots up when we watch a video or see a post we like – and to even higher levels when we get a like or a good comment on a post. There's an even bigger boost when a child completes a level of a video game.

So, the social media algorithm is designed to show us content that keeps us scrolling. Over time, it notices what sort of post gets your attention, and what sort of post would be okay for you to skip or even turn off your phone. It will show you more and more content that's more likely to keep you scrolling. YouTube will keep on showing videos that make your child more likely to keep watching.

Video game designers look at levels where people stop playing and make less of those and make more levels that keep people playing (and spending money). They have to hit the sweet spot of being difficult enough to be challenging (so people fork over money for gems and upgrades), but not so difficult that people give up altogether. And different games would have different thresholds for this, whether it's a complicated game meant for teenagers and adults, to games and apps targeted at young kids.

Again, this isn't some conspiracy theory. These aren't evil people out to destroy the world. They're simply people doing their jobs well and practicing good business sense. We're sacrificing our kids on the altar of commercialism, and our kids are paying the price.

Even with "parental controls," the entire burden of controlling and managing kids' screen time rests on the parents. And because of the algorithm and the dopamine system of our brains, things are stacked up against us. Our "willpower" is no match for all these factors that combine to make screen time seem so easy and appealing while limiting it practically impossible.

That's why, for the story of Lily, I told her she's not a bad parent. No parent wants their child to become a screen time addict. Every parent wants the best for their child. But we're placed in such tough circumstances that it can feel like you need to go live under a rock just to control your child's screen time.

What makes this more challenging is that we're losing nature and places where kids can play. So many kids are cooped up indoors for most of their time. Parents can download entire stacks of "activities for kids" and buy roomfuls of toys, but in the end screen time ends up still being the more appealing option while they're stuck at home.

The Triple Threat of Excessive Screen Time

Excessive screen time can have a triple-threat impact on children. Firstly, it can destroy the parent-child connection. It's difficult to truly connect and communicate when screens are constantly present.

Observational studies have shown that screen time use affects how sensitive and responsive parents are to their babies and kids.[34] And as we've talked about in this book, the responsiveness of the parent or caregiver is

---

[34] Braune-Krickau K, Schneebeli L, Pehlke-Milde J, Gemperle M, Koch R, von Wyl A. Smartphones in the nursery: Parental smartphone use and parental sensitivity and responsiveness within parent-child interaction in early childhood (0-5 years): A scoping review. Infant Ment Health J. 2021 Mar;42(2):161-175. doi: 10.1002/imhj.21908. Epub 2021 Jan 15. PMID: 33452702; PMCID: PMC8048888.

extremely important for brain development in early childhood. The child's entire future – entire early relational health that has lifelong implications – is based on whether they had a responsive caregiver during these early years!

One study showed that high screen time in mothers was associated with conduct problems, symptoms of hyperactivity/inattention, and emotional problems among their children.[35]

Another study observed interactions at a restaurant. The researchers noted that the more time a caregiver spent primarily interacting with a device rather than with the child, the more the children resorted to escalating disruptive behaviors to get the parent's attention. Highly absorbed caregivers were also more likely to respond harshly to misbehavior.

Secondly, screen time can impair a child's ability to regulate their emotions and behavior. Large-scale research has linked early screen time to increased hyperactivity at age 3 as well as emotional and behavioral problems at age 4.[36]

Furthermore, screen time can prime the brain for aggression as it can lead to an increase in the production of the stress hormone cortisol. This can make children more prone to tantrums, meltdowns, and aggressive behavior.

Finally, what children learn from screens is another concern. Many games and apps marketed to children feature violence, explosions, and weapons, normalizing aggression and violence as a form of entertainment – sacrificing our kids' future in the name of likes and views.

---

[35] Poulain T, Ludwig J, Hiemisch A, Hilbert A, Kiess W. Media Use of Mothers, Media Use of Children, and Parent-Child Interaction Are Related to Behavioral Difficulties and Strengths of Children. Int J Environ Res Public Health. 2019 Nov 22;16(23):4651. doi: 10.3390/ijerph16234651. PMID: 31766650; PMCID: PMC6926547.

[36] Wu JB, Yin XN, Qiu SY, Wen GM, Yang WK, Zhang JY, Zhao YF, Wang X, Hong XB, Lu D, Jing J. Association between screen time and hyperactive behaviors in children under 3 years in China. Front Psychiatry. 2022 Nov 9;13:977879. doi: 10.3389/fpsyt.2022.977879. PMID: 36440411; PMCID: PMC9683344. and Liu, W., Wu, X., Huang, K. *et al.* Early childhood screen time as a predictor of emotional and behavioral problems in children at 4 years: a birth cohort study in China. *Environ Health Prev Med* **26**, 3 (2021)

Practical Ways to Manage Screen Time

The first step in managing screen time is to establish clear boundaries and expectations as a family. This means setting limits on how much screen time is allowed each day, as well as when and where screens can be used.

You may also want to keep track of your child's screen time by using apps or built-in device features that track usage, or to have a sand-timer that shows your child visually how much time they have left. Other ways of keeping track are ticking off the number of episodes or videos a child watches.

Apply the other strategies in this book to screen time as well. Connect with them through offline activities. Decide how much screen time your child will be allowed each day and communicate this to them clearly and consistently.

One effective strategy is to create a schedule for screen time. This can include limiting the times when a child is allowed to turn on the television. I recommend using a television that a parent controls and where you can see what's going on, rather than a hand-held device such as a phone or tablet that the child controls. (All this is part of creating a Family Media Use Plan, as recommended by the American Academy of Pediatrics.)[37]

Co-viewing (watching with your child) can help minimize the harmful effects of screen time,[38] and co-viewing will be much easier with television than with a smaller device.

---

[37] https://www.healthychildren.org/English/family-life/Media/Pages/default.aspx
[38] Canadian Paediatric Society, Digital Health Task Force, Ottawa, Ontario. Screen time and young children: Promoting health and development in a digital world. Paediatr Child Health. 2017 Nov;22(8):461-477. doi: 10.1093/pch/pxx123. Epub 2017 Oct 9. Erratum in: Paediatr Child Health. 2018 Feb;23 (1):83. PMID: 29601064; PMCID: PMC5823000. and Latomme J, Van Stappen V, Cardon G, Morgan PJ, Lateva M, Chakarova N, Kivelä J, Lindström J, Androutsos O, González-Gil EM, De Miguel-Etayo P, Nánási A, Kolozsvári LR, Manios Y, De Craemer M. The Association between Children's and Parents' Co-TV Viewing and Their Total Screen Time in Six European Countries: Cross-Sectional Data from the Feel4diabetes-Study. Int J Environ Res Public Health. 2018 Nov 21;15(11):2599. doi: 10.3390/ijerph15112599. PMID: 30469348; PMCID: PMC6266975

Another important consideration is the quality of screen time. This is my beef with a lot of the top results on YouTube Kids. Many parents think that just because it's on YouTube Kids, it's okay for kids to watch.

Now, most parents are surprised to learn that there's no "rating organization" that decides if something is okay for kids to watch. Do you know how YouTube decides whether something is okay for kids or not? (You may know this already, but I include this here because so many people are surprised when I tell them this! I didn't know this myself until I started a YouTube channel.) When someone uploads a video, there's a checkbox that asks, "Is this video made for kids?" If you check that box, then it's considered for kids! That's it! It's the *video creator* – not an objective third party (unlike the rating organizations we have for network television) that decides whether something is for kids! *Anyone* can upload *anything* and say it's for kids.

Of course, if there's something truly objectionable, parents who see it will complain to YouTube. YouTube will review the content and it may be removed. But how many kids will have seen this in the meantime? (You've probably heard stories of downright inappropriate content on YouTube Kids. Personally, there was this time my son and his cousins were watching what they thought was "Thomas and Friends" – until we noticed it was a scary-looking Thomas, guns and bombs were exploding in the background, and loads of people getting electrocuted.) This is why, more than ever, we need to be extremely vigilant about what our kids watch.

Back to the top shows on YouTube Kids. Remember what I said about the algorithm and our brain's dopamine system? Fast-paced videos, with a lot of fast animations and changing scenes, tend to be more engaging and give our brains a bigger dopamine boost. They excite our brains more and condition our brains to this level of stimulation. So, these are also the videos that kids are more likely to watch – so they get shown to more and more kids, and that's why they're the top videos. NOT because they're better. A lot of videos that show up at the top results for "educational videos" are overstimulating and do NOT fit the criteria for "high quality" shows.

When people say, "Screen time isn't bad. Some research shows screen time is beneficial for kids." These studies talk about shows like Sesame Street (one research showed benefits for kids who watched Sesame Street in the 1960s[39]) or shows such as Daniel Tiger and Mister Roger's Neighborhood.

But how much time do kids spend watching shows like these today? Even "educational" shows have oversaturated colors, fast animations, and shapes or numbers flashing all over the screen and bouncing back and forth. These videos condition the child's brain to a level of stimulation that isn't reasonable to expect in real life.

So, when you choose screen time for your child, *don't* simply search for "educational videos for toddlers." Instead, look at the video. Here's what to look for:

- Slower pace – same pace as real life. I know, these are the "boring" videos. They'll never make it to the top of search results.

- No fast scene changes or fast animations. These fast animation videos are now flooding YouTube Kids. Do you know why? Because it's so easy to create these using artificial intelligence! AI can create the video script, make the animations, and everything from the title and description that push it to the top of the search results (and AI can even narrate it). AI can churn these videos out in bulk, so the channel gets more views and makes more money. So if you see an animated video with the title "Teach Your Child the Numbers 1-10," you have no idea whether it was even reviewed by a human who understands how kids learn numbers, or whether the whole thing was created by AI because it's one of the top searches.

- Videos of real people are better than animated videos. Find videos of real kids dancing at a normal pace, singing, exercising, or doing arts and crafts. Or videos of real people reading books (not just the

---

[39] https://www.wellesley.edu/sites/default/files/assets/site/files/wellesleysesamestudy_full.pdf

animated version of a book) or having face-to-face conversations with each other.

- Audio-only apps are great! Instead of using the animated video of your child's favorite nursery rhyme, put on an audio playlist. Instead of an animated book, put on the audiobook. Many short audiobooks are engaging for kids.

These are easier to enforce if your child's brain hasn't been conditioned to require faster animations. That's one of the reasons why we recommend delaying introducing screen time.

I notice that often, parents who introduce screen time to babies before 18 months start out choosing the right kind of screen time.

But then the algorithm takes over and keeps pushing more engaging videos with fast animations. Before long, the child demands more and more exciting videos until nothing short of a fast paced and overstimulating video can satisfy them.

This is exactly what happened with Lily and other parents like her! They started with wonderful intentions, but the algorithm combined with the effect of screen time on the dopamine system made it practically impossible to draw the line.

That's why I recommend using a television and then controlling what the child sees. An alternative is to download videos you've pre-selected, then turn off the internet access (this assumes your child hasn't figured out how to turn it on)! Then – and this is a very important step – you also need to turn off automatic downloads. You also need to remember to turn this off each time your device receives an update!

I learned this from personal experience. I'd downloaded a bunch of Sesame Street videos – with the occasional Paw Patrol – for my child to watch. I turned off the Wi-Fi, turned off automatic downloads, then gave the iPad to my son for him to watch while I worked, smug in the knowledge that he's watching only approved shows.

When I returned after 30 minutes, lo and behold – he was watching a very popular cartoon (which I won't name) that had heroes and villains shooting each other every few seconds! I soon discovered that even if I had turned off the Wi-Fi *and* automatic downloads, each time the iPad receives an update, these automatic downloads populate themselves all over again!

Create screen-free zones. Designate certain areas of your home, such as the dining table or bedrooms, as screen-free zones. This will help promote family time and reduce screen time.

It's also important to **model healthy screen behavior** yourself. Set aside time each day for non-screen activities, such as reading, playing outside, or engaging in a hobby.

I know this is easier said than done, especially if (like me) your work involves being online. You're the best person to decide exactly how to do this. What works for me is explaining to my child that what I'm doing is for work (and he does see me working on the website or typing this book away on a word processor), and he also sees me putting gadgets away.

Also, before I became a parent, I'd been reading mostly e-books. But after I became a parent, I consciously decided to get more print books because I wanted my child to see me reading print books and doing offline activities.

Finally, it's important to have open and honest communication with your child about the importance of managing screen time. Explain to them the potential negative effects of excessive screen time and the benefits of limiting their screen use.

A few months ago, I met up with a college friend I haven't seen in over two decades. It struck me how her eleven-year-old son is so mature, respectful, and grounded. He's a genuinely happy kid who followed our conversation and added his thoughtful ideas. He talked with my child too and was like a kind and helpful big brother.

And last month, I attended the birthday party of a friend's daughter. It struck me how her two daughters were both articulate while being kind and polite at the same time. They were genuinely happy people who patiently played with my son and got along with their friends. I knew they had excellent critical thinking skills, because at that time I was working on a journal for kids that I was publishing, and I asked their opinion. Their

> Rather than making a child unable to cope with technology, limiting screen time allows kids to explore more creative and productive uses of technology. It allows them to learn to *use* technology, rather than being controlled by it

thoughtful comments helped me improve the journal.

What did they have in common? These were two families from different countries across the world, coming from different cultures, with parents in diverse professions and diverse personalities. The one thing they had in common was – *very strict* screen time limits.

Yet another family I know – a family of seven, no less! – also has a strict screen time policy, and I see the huge impact this has made on their family relationships, and how the kids are quite responsible, with the siblings looking after each other.

They were allowed screen time for homework or creative pursuits, but they could watch only an hour or two of video on weekends. They did not do online gaming. The eleven-year-old boy I mentioned writes articles for his blog, while the daughters I mentioned create their own designs in Canva. The eldest child that I mentioned was even selected for an international robotics competition.

I'm sharing these not to make anyone feel guilty if they don't enforce limits like these. But I wanted to share these examples of how, rather than making a child unable to cope with technology, limiting screen time allows kids to explore more creative and productive uses of technology. It allows them to learn to *use* technology, rather than being controlled by it.

As I write this, there are rapid changes in the field of artificial intelligence that might make it even more difficult to control screen time. More research continues to be published. Be sure to head over to discerningparenting.com/behavior where I'll keep this section updated.

CHAPTER 8

TAKING CARE OF YOU

In a "State of Motherhood Survey" conducted in 2021 by Motherly, 93% of Moms reported feeling burned out, and 43% felt completely burned out. In 2022, Moms who reported feeling completely burned out went down to 38% – slightly better but still high![40]

Maybe you've been thinking –

I'm capable and successful. Why do I feel like I'm failing at parenting?

Maybe you're feeling tired, worn out, stressed, or guilty. Maybe others are criticizing your parenting. You're working so hard and trying to do everything and yet it feels like it's never enough.

The thing is, with all these stresses, a lot of the expectations and the parenting advice we hear are quite "ideal." There's this expectation on us to be the Supermom who can do everything all the time for kids and the entire family.

Not to mention that parents often get little sympathy from others if their struggles are related to a child's behavior.

If a parent stays up all night because a child had a fever and a stuffy nose, most people can empathize. Only the most insensitive people will blame the parent.

---

[40] https://www.mother.ly/news/2021-state-of-motherhood-survey/

https://www.mother.ly/news/2022-state-of-motherhood-survey/#pandemic-burnout-may-be-waning-but-not-enough

But that's not the case for a parent who feels completely spent after dealing with an hour-long meltdown, chasing a hyperactive toddler the entire afternoon, or nearly the entire day playing referee between fighting siblings.

Despite all the evidence that behavior problems do have a biological basis, parents who struggle with their kids' behavior problems are often accused of having created their own problems. "It's because you're spoiling them." "It's because you don't discipline them enough."

I saw a study that said being a Mom is like working 2.5 full-time jobs – but sometimes it can feel like 8.5 jobs!

I know what it feels like to be so exhausted that I felt as if I didn't have a single ounce of energy to give. To be stretched so thin that even the slightest negative comment can set me off.

And isn't it funny that some people choose that moment to "sympathetically" say things like, "You look horrible!" Then follow up with, "It's because you're so stressed. Just calm down." I know they mean well, but I felt like shouting, *If I knew how to calm down don't you think I'd be doing it already?!*

This chapter is about taking care of you and handling parental burnout, but I realize no chapter on this topic will ever, on its own, solve the problem.

A lot has been written about "you should do self-care as a parent." But each situation is different. Some are dealing with a death in the family. Some have lost their jobs and are working so hard to make ends meet. Some may even be trapped in an abusive situation.

For many people, "Just do self-care" doesn't cut it. There needs to be *actual* change in the circumstances and support in doing so.

It's also not true that practicing self-care and avoiding burnout means that we need to be happy and calm all the time.

We're conditioned to believe that being happy is "good," and being sad or upset is "bad." We're often told, "Just think positive!" Or "It's all in your head! It's all about attitude!" We may end up suppressing what we perceive as "bad" emotions until we reach our breaking point, then explode.

Leah Kuypers in her theory *Zones of Regulation* classifies emotions as "zones" rather than good or bad. Each emotion has its place.

Feeling sad does *not* mean that we love our kids any less. Feeling tired and exhausted and wishing we had less work does *not* mean we're any less grateful for the blessings we have.

Social media has conditioned us to have a narrow view of self-care that's all about getting pedicures or spa massages. This has made busy parents believe that it's impossible to do self-care and that it's a luxury. Or they may put it off for "when things aren't so busy" or "when the kids are in school the whole day."

But self-care is not something you do only if everything is going well. When things are going wrong, all the more you need self-care.

Self-care is NOT selfish. We've heard time and again about the airplane analogy. At the safety briefing at the start of every flight, the flight attendant always says, "If you're with a child, attend to yourself first before attending to the child."

In one of the courses I took for my Parent Coaching Certification, our trainer said, "The lioness feeds herself first. Because she knows her cubs will not survive without her!"

Self-care is NOT something that others pressure you into doing. It's not something that you need to spend for. There's no pressure around it.

But if we want to teach our kids emotional regulation and resilience, we need to be okay. I know how tough it will be to practice the principles in this book if a parent isn't mentally healthy. What can we do as parents?

Take Care of Your Health

Eat healthy food. Get enough exercise. Drink enough water. Get enough sleep. Get enough sunlight exposure for Vitamin D. I understand how, to many busy parents, these may sound like, "Geez, I know that, but I just don't have the time."

But every bit you do will help. Whether it's by doing them along with your child or letting go of some commitments, know that you won't be able to help your child and your family at all if you get sick.

Check out the Discerning Parenting podcast, where Wayne State University-trained psychiatrist Dr. Julie Arellano-Khullar shares with us how important these "basics" like food and sleep are in parental mental health, as well as practical tips. We link to the episode in your bonus material.

Give Time and Space for You

This sounds obvious. It sounds easy to say but difficult to do – but hear me out.

Here I'll share a bit of my journey. I've been helping parents for over a decade. I've also taught medical students and pediatricians-in-training about how to help parents with baby and childcare.

So, parenting should have been a breeze for me, right? WRONG!!! I'm ashamed to say I would lose my temper at home. I was trying to accommodate everyone and everything, getting more and more tired. I was trying to do too much, and I did not know how to stop.

I had the knowledge. I knew what I should be focusing on, but I didn't have the confidence to actually apply it. And I realized something was missing.

So, I went through an intense subconscious healing journey. I learned to truly believe that I was enough. I gained the confidence to focus.

I learned to enjoy the moment instead of always thinking of what I had to do next. Because that's how many of us are programmed. We're programmed to always be doing something. We can't rest unless all our things to do are done – but that never happens!

Making time and space for you doesn't have to be this big vacation away from kids. (Though if you want to and you have the means to do so, go ahead and don't feel guilty about it!)

Research has shown even 15 minutes of meditation can replicate the benefits of taking a whole day's vacation.[41]

Brief, daily meditative journeys enhance attention, memory, mood, and emotional regulation – even in those with no prior experience of meditation. They can help us be more patient and help us show more empathy toward others – and we definitely need patience and empathy as parents![42]

---

[41] https://www.tandfonline.com/doi/full/10.1080/17439760.2019.1610480
[42] https://www.sciencedirect.com/science/article/abs/pii/S016643281830322X?via%3Dihub

That's why this book includes this very important self-care chapter. And this is why my parent coaching includes a meditative journey as part of the experience. Because simply knowing the strategies may not be enough. We all know that when we're stressed, these strategies and all our best intentions can fly out the window!

Be Clear About Goals and Priorities

What are the things that are important to us? Focus on that. Don't let social media make you feel guilty. Sometimes as Moms, we feel pressured to do things that we don't need or want to do, because of what we see on social media. Hopefully, this book has helped you discern what your goals and priorities are too.

Give Your Kids Age-Appropriate Tasks

Don't try to do everything. Don't try to solve all your kids' problems. Don't feel pressured to entertain your kids all the time.

Let's All Support Each Other

Fighting burnout isn't just about self-care – but it's also about having a village. Instead of asking, "How can I manage to do everything all by myself?" It may be better to ask, "What can I do so I get the help and support I need?"

I know this can sound like wishful thinking, but I hope our society also becomes more supportive of parenting.

We may need to let others know how to support us. The bonuses that come with this book include a printable sheet you can use to let others know what you need. Be sure to head over to discerningparenting.com/behavior.

Seek professional help if needed. Seeking professional help is not a sign of weakness, and you do not have to do it all on your own.

It's Okay to Say No

Often, we don't like saying no because we may be afraid of disappointing others. We need to give ourselves permission to say no. Have a prepared script for saying no so it's easier. You don't need to give a reason.

We only have 24 hours in a day. Each time we say yes to something, we're really saying no to all the other things that we could have done in that same amount of time.

This is something I had to realize. Before, when someone asked me for a favor, I would think, "Why not? That sounds like a nice thing to do." Until I realized that doing that "nice thing" meant skipping out on meals, sleep, exercise, time with my family, prayer, or any number of other things. And it was not until I went on a deep healing journey to trust myself did I have the courage to say no to many demands on my time.

> Each time we say yes to something, we're really saying no to all the other things that we could have done in that same amount of time.

Remember that if you keep saying yes to other people, you'll be sacrificing yourself, your health, and your kids. Ask yourself if it's worth it. I think the pandemic made many of us reflect on and revamp our priorities, and we all realized that we're not helping anyone if we stretch ourselves so thin that we get sick ourselves.

Yes, it is good to help others. But this does not mean we need to take on the problems of everyone we encounter, nor does this mean we need to say yes to every favor that others ask from us. If you're sleeping only five hours every night or skipping meals or feeling exhausted all the time that you're already snapping at your kids, you shouldn't feel that you have to say yes to that "teeny tiny favor that will take only a few minutes." (I'm sure you know from experience that those "teeny tiny favors" have a way of adding up!)

Pray

Make time to pray and practice your faith or spirituality. There's growing evidence on the positive relationship between spirituality, mental health, and positive well-being.

Know That It's Okay to Be Exhausted

It was one of those days. I'd collapsed on the play mat after nearly 20 hours of being on my feet.

If my son hadn't tapped me on the shoulder, saying "Mommy, get up," I might have stayed that way the entire night.

As I was staring up at the ceiling, trying to will myself to get up, it reminded me of three things that one hears when we are brave enough or honestly, just so exhausted that we let the words "I'm tired" spill from our mouths.

> #1 - *"All you need to do" advice.*
>> "All you need to do is lock the door and rest." (Even if your child is crying outside and banging on the door.)
>>
>> "All you need to do is have a routine."
>>
>> "All you need to do is sleep train."
>>
>> ...and things will be fine.

You'll see this on social media. "Do this one thing and end your parenting challenges forever." Or even in books. I remember seeing a blurb that said, "This book will solve all your parenting problems!"

> #2 - *"Why did you"/"Why didn't you" questions*
>> "Why did you take on that project?"
>>
>> "Why didn't you nap while your toddler was napping?"
>>
>> "Why didn't you ask for help?"

> #3 - *"At least you ...." statements*
>> "At least you have people to help you."
>>
>> "At least you can focus on your kids." (Often said to stay-at-home or work-from-home Moms)

> "At least you can get a breather while you're at work instead of parenting 24/7." (Often said to Moms who work a 9-5)

They may be well-meaning. Maybe they're helpful and maybe they're not. But parenting isn't that simple. There's no one simple solution that will work for everyone all the time.

That's why this book – and all our resources at Discerning Parenting – were created with the understanding that for every parenting question, there are so many nuances around it.

And created by someone who knows what it is like when "100% works every time" and "end your struggles forever!" strategies don't work the way the books or social media posts say they should.

When that happens, this doesn't mean we're failing as parents. This doesn't mean we don't have any hope of things getting better.

So, if you're one tired Mama who's tired of hearing people insist that it's all your fault when you're feeling tired, know that you're not alone.

Head over to discerningparenting.com/behavior. Along with your bonus materials, you can also learn more about how the Discerning Parenting community can support you further.

CHAPTER 9

WHEN IS IT MORE THAN "JUST THE TERRIBLE TWOS"?

It was as if a wild animal was loose in the church. A young child, around the age of five, was running around and making strange noises like a wild animal. His mom kept calling him to either sit down or run in the garden outside, but to no avail. She was mortified, feeling the stares of the churchgoers as they saw her locked in a power struggle with her son.

The child, Aidan, was almost always running around, jumping, shouting, disrespecting the adults, and getting into fights with the other kids. Aidan's mom was frequently told, "All he needs is a spanking, and he'll never do that again!"

But she'd heard of a younger brother of her colleague who seemed similar to Aidan. That younger brother was frequently spanked but never learned to "behave," so they had to spank him harder and harder, and more and more frequently.

Aidan's mom wonders, "Is it really 'just a lack of discipline' - or maybe a prolonged case of the 'terrible two's' - or is there something more?"

Are my child's tantrums normal? Should I worry?

Is it really "just the terrible twos" – the "threenager" phase – or is it something more?

My child hits and kicks – is this just a phase they'll outgrow, or do I need to do something about it?

When is it more than "just the terrible twos"? (And this does NOT in any way diminish the terrible twos or the "threenager phase" – that can last beyond age three!)

These are among the most common questions I get. Tantrums and behavior that hurts others are among the most common reasons why a child would be brought to a developmental and behavioral pediatrician.

Typically, by the time parents bring their child to see us, they've been through a lot of stress. They've questioned themselves and felt like bad parents. They've received different pieces of advice that may have left them more and more confused.

They've heard, "Don't worry, that's just the terrible twos. They'll outgrow it!" Or "All you need to do is validate their feelings!"

They've also heard, "If you don't punish them now so they know it's wrong, you'll have a huge problem when your child is a teenager and is still having tantrums!"

Then there are the fear messages (mostly used to sell something). I even saw an ad on Facebook – supposedly by a "parenting and neuroscience expert" – that said, "Tantrums cause irreversible damage to your child's brain!" (When I Googled the studies that were mentioned, *all these studies were about adverse childhood experiences. NONE of them were about tantrums.* For more about protecting your child's brain – that's accurate and NOT fearmongering, head over to discerningparenting.com/behavior).

So typically, when it comes to behavior problems, I notice that the advice parents get tends to fall into one of two categories.

Category 1 – Don't worry about problem behaviors. They're absolutely normal. Sometimes, they follow up with "all you need to do" advice. ("All you need to do is be more consistent." "All you need to do is set firmer limits.") OR

Category 2 – No way! They're not normal behaviors – in fact, the child is bad and naughty and if the parents don't spank or punish the naughtiness out of them immediately, they're doomed. (Or occasionally, you just need to buy their course or product otherwise your child is doomed).

Compared to language or developmental delays where people may realize that they need a medical consultation, it's rare that someone actually considers this when it comes to behavior problems. But if you look at the factors behind challenging behavior from Chapter 1, they *do* stem from what goes on – physically – in a child's brain!

Only when the kids are in school (sometimes already in the older grade levels) and the teachers note aggressive or disruptive behavior, that's the only time they're referred to us. By that time, these kids have already suffered years of being labeled as "bad" and it's already ingrained in their beliefs of who they are.

Signs You May Need to Seek Professional Help with Your Child's Challenging Behavior

Remember, even without these signs, anytime you're worried, you can seek professional help. We do see that even kids who end up not receiving any diagnosis still benefit from intervention. **All families can benefit from parenting support.**

As we noted earlier in this book, not all challenging behavior is abnormal.

A lot of toddler behaviors that adults don't like (like running around, saying no, and exploring everything) – are *normal* developmental milestones.

Some difficulty dealing with frustration is also normal since young kids are still learning.

And there are a lot of other behaviors that may simply be the result of expectations that are too advanced, such as tantrums when a three-year-old is asked to sit at a table and answer worksheets.

But here are some signs that you may need to seek consultation about your child's behavior. None of this is meant to cause alarm. If one of these signs is present, it does NOT mean that there's something wrong with your child or that you've failed as a parent.

But we point this out because there are times when extra help and support may be needed to help handle your toddler's behavior. The earlier we start helping your child, the better the outcomes.

Early intervention *does* work. It can prevent more serious behavioral problems from developing and can improve outcomes for children in the long term.

Communication Delays

Delays in language and communication can make behavior problems more likely. For more about this, check my first book, "Toddler Talking," where I include a chapter on what to do if you're worried that your child might have speech and language delay.[43]

Language skills are extremely important in regulating emotions.[44] *All* toddlers, whether or not they have a speech delay, are still developing their language skills. This makes toddlers more prone to tantrums. That may be the only way they know of expressing their feelings. They may not yet have the vocabulary to say they are hungry, tired, or overwhelmed.

Kids with speech delays have an even harder time with emotional regulation. A recent study[45] showed that two-year-olds who can say less than 50 words are twice as likely to have frequent and severe tantrums.

That's why we need to watch out for behavior problems that are associated with speech delay. If your child has a speech delay, she needs help as soon as possible. The toddler years are a critical period for language development. We don't want to miss out on the chance to intervene early if there is a problem.

---

[43] https://discerningparenting.com/two-year-old-babbling-but-not-yet-talking/
[44] https://thoughtfulparent.com/language-skills-help-boys-develop-self.html
[45] https://www.parents.com/news/late-talkers-more-tantrums/

Frequent Or Repetitive Aggressive Behavior That Happens in Multiple Settings

Kicking and biting once in a while – maybe while frustrated or sleepy – might just be part of this age. However, frequent kicking and biting in different situations and multiple settings (at home, at the playground, and in daycare) may need to be evaluated.

Parents often ask, "How frequent is frequent?"

The Early Intervention Group of Northwestern University is conducting an excellent and very interesting study about this, called the "When to Worry Study."[46] They conducted specific and objective assessments about toddler tantrums, using standardized tests. The study authors recommend watching out for tantrums that are "intense, prolonged, or unpredictable."

Toddlers usually have short tantrums as frequently as once a day, with most of them lasting less than five minutes.[47] There may be longer tantrums once in a while, but these shouldn't happen too often. While there is no hard and fast rule, when a child's usual tantrum lasts longer than 25 minutes, it may be a cause for concern.

But more than having a specific number, it's more important to ask, "How is it affecting your *functioning*?" How is it affecting your daily life?

If your child kicks and bites so often that you're already avoiding the playground and you already find playdates exhausting, or it's a struggle to get through your daily activities, then it's already affecting functioning.

---

[46] https://news.northwestern.edu/stories/2018/february/the-science-of-when-to-worry/
[47] https://pubmed.ncbi.nlm.nih.gov/12806226/

Age-Inappropriate Behavior

After the toddler years, kids typically shouldn't be having daily tantrums anymore. One research in children who are 3-6 years old found that those who have more than 20 tantrums a month were more likely to have psychological problems.[48] Those who have difficulty recovering from a tantrum are also at increased risk.

Running around and having difficulty sitting at a table and staying still may still be normal for a toddler or even a preschooler. But as the child grows older, they should be able to sit for gradually longer periods. A 3-4-year-old who is still constantly running around and is unable to sit for a meal or to complete an age-appropriate activity may need to be evaluated.

Associated Problems with Social Skills

As parents, we often worry about when our kids should be learning things like the alphabet and numbers. However, these are not the most important skills to learn during the toddler years. At this age, **it is even more important that they learn age-appropriate social skills**.

Many people don't realize the social aspect of behavior! These are early signs of possible problems with social skills.

- By 12 months at the latest, if you point out something interesting to your child, she should be able to follow and look at where you point.
- By the time your child is 15 months old, he should be pointing at things that he wants. When he is 18 months, he should also be pointing at things not only because he wants them, but simply because they interest him.

---

[48] https://pubmed.ncbi.nlm.nih.gov/12806226/

- Your child should be imitating what the people around her do or say by the time she is 2 years old, and playing pretend games by the time she is 3.[49]

Just like with language, your child will need help if there are problems with social skills. Toddlers learn to regulate their emotions through a process called **co-regulation**. This means that **they need warm and responsive interaction with us** to be able to deal with these big feelings that trigger tantrums.

That's why developing social skills is a very important part of how a child learns appropriate behavior. If your child finds it very difficult to interact with others, it can lead to behavior challenges.

Being shy around others or needing time to get used to new people or places is generally normal at this age. However, these are some signs that an evaluation may be needed:

- not responding to their name or not making eye contact with other people
- not being interested in other kids
- acting fearful in most social situations
- appearing unaware of others and what's going on

Even very young toddlers should already be aware of what's going on around them. If they're not, this can lead to a lot of behavior that's misinterpreted as aggression – such as bumping into or hitting others because they simply didn't realize they were there.

If a child's behavior is affecting their ability to play or socialize with others, it may be time to seek help.

---

[49] Check out the CDC Milestone Tracker App of the CDC website here for the updated developmental milestones. https://www.cdc.gov/ncbddd/actearly/index.html

Concerns Over Mental Health

Toddlers don't express anxiety or depression the way adults do. A toddler who's feeling depressed may not necessarily cry or act sad, and an anxious toddler may not look like they're fearful. Instead, they may act out by punching, kicking, or hurting others. These cues are often missed!

Frequent Aggression When Gadgets Are Taken Away

In our practice, we frequently encounter children who become aggressive when gadgets are taken away, or when there's a lag in the internet connection.

It is normal to have an occasional tantrum over screen time. However, if it's extremely difficult for you to set limits on screen time, this may be a warning sign.

If a child consistently has tantrums or acts aggressively each time you take away a gadget, or if the child shows no interest at all in screen-free activities,[50] it may be time to seek help on this. These are signs of possible internet addiction for which professional help may be needed.

We've worked with parents who say it's practically impossible to enforce limits on screen time.[51] Their toddlers act violently by kicking, screaming, biting, and hitting when they try to engage them in screen-free activities. Only a tablet or phone can pacify them.

If this is the situation, simple willpower or simply telling yourself, "Okay, someday I'll work harder and limit gadgets" may not be enough.

We have seen internet addiction all too often in older children and even in adults. Unfortunately, we are starting to see this more often in toddlers too.

Remember, anytime you're concerned, it's okay to seek help. Even if your child doesn't have a diagnosis, you may still need support.

It's Not "All in The Head"!

A number of medical conditions may lead to challenging behaviors. These include being in the autism spectrum, sensory processing difficulties, and attention deficit – hyperactivity disorder.

---

[50] https://childmind.org/article/is-internet-addiction-real/
[51]

Quite often too, a child is brought to our clinics for behavior problems, and it turns out there are undiagnosed language or developmental delays.

Learning disorders are also quite common. Many times, we get these kids when they are already in fourth or fifth grade or even later, and they've been labeled "naughty" or "lazy" all their lives. When we evaluate them, it turns out they have a learning disorder. That's why there have been so many challenges in school and when doing homework – and they've been acting out because of these challenges.

We don't call a child with asthma "naughty" if he can't breathe because we know that there's an actual underlying physical cause. In the same way, we can't call a child with ADHD "naughty" if he won't stay still. There is an underlying physical cause and an actual difference in the brain that can be measured in brain studies. Instead of labeling, we need to help them.

Disorders such as seizures may also present as challenging behaviors. Since I did my pediatric residency at a tertiary referral hospital where all the "rare" cases go, we also saw instances when a previously well-behaved child suddenly started having more tantrums and difficult behavior, and it turned out to be something that needs medical attention.

Whether or not it turns out there's a medical diagnosis, *all* families will benefit from parental support. It's a misconception that you need support only if your child has an outright diagnosis. That's why I'm passionate about providing parenting coaching.

What To Do If You're Worried or If You Notice These Warning Signs

If there are warning signs for behavior problems, it's never too early to seek help. Early intervention works and it's easier because the negative experiences and labels haven't set in. We don't want to wait until your child has already been labeled "bad" by everyone around them – including themselves.

The actual process to get support will be different depending on where you are. In some places, you can go straight to seeing a developmental pediatrician. In other places, you need to get a referral from your primary care provider before being seen by a specialist. In some places, medical professionals may not be heavily involved in evaluating and managing children with behavior problems, but instead, these are done by teachers, psychologists, and parent coaches.

In general, though, the process would include at least some of these steps.

Developmental and Behavioral Screening and Surveillance by Your Pediatrician

Each time you go to your pediatrician for a check-up, your pediatrician does what we call *developmental surveillance*. Your pediatrician may check which developmental milestones your child has reached and will also observe your child's behavior at the clinic.

This is why it's important not to miss well-baby and well-child check-ups. If your pediatrician doesn't see your child other than when there's a high fever (and your child is irritable), they won't be able to observe your child's "usual" behavior well.

Your pediatrician may also ask you to complete questionnaires about your child's development and behavior. This is called *developmental screening*. Your pediatrician may do this at specific ages (usually at 9 months, 18 or 24 months, 30 months, and at 4-5 years or before school entry).[52] If there are any concerns identified during developmental surveillance, your pediatrician will also do developmental screening, regardless of your child's age.

Screening test results usually fall into one of these three categories:

1. For many children, the screening will show that development is on track, and the pediatrician will provide what we call "anticipatory guidance." This means they will help you deal with common questions and do preventive care. For behavior, "anticipatory guidance" may cover things like managing screen time.
2. For some children, there might be some concerns that we need to observe more closely. If this is the case, your pediatrician may give advice specific to your situation and what you can do.

---

[52] https://www.aap.org/en/patient-care/developmental-surveillance-and-screening-patient-care/

You'll be asked to return (usually within 3 months) for a repeat screening. If there are still problems with the repeat screening, then you'll be referred to a specialist for further evaluation.

3. Other children may show signs that they need to be evaluated right away, in which case you'll be referred to a specialist.

Referral To Specialists

Many parents have asked me who would be the best professional to see if their child has behavior problems. Should they see a "dev peds," a child psychiatrist, a child psychologist, or another professional? What's the difference?

Here are the professionals who frequently work with kids who have behavior problems (this is not an exhaustive list).

A developmental and behavioral pediatrician (often called a "dev peds") is a medical doctor who completed residency training in pediatrics after medical school and then went on to have special training in developmental and behavioral pediatrics afterward.

A child psychiatrist is also a medical doctor. They completed residency training in psychiatry, then went on to have special training in child psychiatry.

A child psychologist, on the other hand, completed a master's or doctorate in child psychology or developmental psychology. There may be different psychologists who work with kids – such as a clinical psychologist, counseling psychologist, or neuropsychologist.

The actual process of evaluating a child with problem behaviors and which of these professionals will see you first may be different in each country. You may first see a developmental pediatrician who will refer you to other specialists, or it may also be the other way around.

Also, it's not unusual to not get a diagnosis right away, or for the diagnosis to evolve as your child grows older.

If you receive a diagnosis, it is normal to go through an entire range of overwhelming emotions. Know that you're not alone in feeling this way.

Remember this – being given a diagnosis related to your child's development, behavior, or mental health does *not* mean you've failed as a parent. In *no way* does it mean that your child's future is doomed.

Your child is still the same wonderful child that you love. They still have all their unique and amazing strengths, and no label or diagnosis can define them.

Intervention

Ideally, intervention already starts even before getting a diagnosis. This is because the *best* intervention for behavior problems is what parents do at home.

Here are some of the common interventions for behavior problems.

Parent Education and Support

Yes, parent training *is* an intervention! The good thing is this can be done even while waiting for a slot to see a professional.

It's important to go through a parent training program that has evidence behind its effectiveness. A lot of "parent training programs" – especially if we look at the internet, are just based on "this is what I did with my child so it should 100% work for everyone else."

So, when vetting a course that promises to help your child behave better, be sure to head over to the About page. If the only credentials you see are personal experiences and stories of others who went through the program "and my child now behaves better!" –I'm not saying these programs are bad, it's just that it may not be all that different from the advice you're already getting from your friends or relatives. They may be valuable for support, but don't assume that just because they're selling a program, that means everything they say is gospel truth.

The best kind of parent training program would be one that has actual research studies that it works. This means they compared parents who took that program with those who did not.

The people at home are the BIGGEST part of an intervention. Not the therapist. If you live in a multigenerational home, others who help take care of your child and whom your child encounters frequently at home will need to be involved.

I know this is easier said than done, especially if everyone disagrees on what should be done (and especially if others at home don't even believe there's a diagnosis, but they think the child is just naughty or spoiled!).

If this is your situation, you may need to discern whether things are likely to improve. For example, are they willing to read this book, attend a parent training program, or implement the changes recommended by your child's therapists? If not, you may need to start considering what options you have for creating a setting where your child can thrive.

Therapy

There are many kinds of therapy for behavior problems.

Where I practice, pediatric occupational therapists are often among the first professionals to work with a child who has behavior problems. In many other countries, a behavior therapist may be one who works with a child the most.

Other programs may include cognitive behavior therapy, play therapy, social skills training, or training in executive function skills or emotional regulation.

Here's what you need to consider when vetting a therapy program:

1. Collaborate with your care provider, such as your developmental and behavioral pediatrician, in making therapy decisions. We're equipped to help you create a holistic plan based on what your child needs. That's why it's important to find a care provider you trust, so you don't get FOMO (or fear of missing out) at every "therapy" that pops up on your Facebook feed.

2. Check the training and licensing credentials. Your care provider will help you with this. I know that it's difficult to find an available slot, and most professionals have long waitlists. Because of this, a lot of programs have popped up that haven't been vetted by research. Parents may join these programs, believing that "something is

better than nothing." That's why parent training is crucial. If you're still waiting for a slot for therapy, for example, it's better to follow an evidence-based parent training program rather than enroll your child in a program with an unlicensed therapist.

3. It's best if the team will collaborate with each other. This works best if your care provider knows about the professionals you're working with, and the professionals know about each other too. Avoid "secretly" enrolling your child in different therapy programs without each therapist knowing about it.

4. Even the best therapy program and the best therapists will have limited results if there's no follow-through at home. Often, I hear the complaint, "The child is like an angel at the therapy center, but there's no improvement in behavior at home and in school!" This is why follow-through is essential. Collaborate with the professionals on your child's team so you know how to carry over the progress at home. This brings me to the next item in intervention, which is school and home support.

Support At Home and In School

Remember earlier in this book when we said that behavior isn't just about the child, but also about the environment? That's why helping kids with behavior problems isn't just about therapy – which is working with the child – but it's also about setting up the environment for better behavior!

A lot of the principles behind this will be similar to the principles we've tackled in this book. Setting up a routine.

Communicating your expectations.

Others would depend on the diagnosis behind the child's behavior challenges. For example, if there are sensory processing issues, special support may need to be in place as well as methods to help your child deal with these.

It's important to choose a school that will recognize and appreciate your child's strengths. Each child – whether they have challenging behaviors – or have strengths that need to be nurtured, each child counts.

In the process of trying to get the child to "behave," we don't want to stamp out the child's creativity and critical thinking. In the process of teaching a child to listen and speak in turn, we don't want the child to end up believing they should never speak up and their ideas aren't welcome.

Find your trusted team to help you. You'll receive so much unsolicited advice and question yourself along the way, so get their support to help you discern what's right for you. Your trusted team can involve the professionals you work with, a good friend for moral support, or people who help you with tasks such as cleaning and laundry.

It takes a village to raise a child. Find your village. Don't try to do it all on your own.

Finally, believe in your child. Notice your child's strengths. Practice the strategies in this book for connecting with your child. This is especially critical in children with behavior challenges.

You will need to advocate for your child. People around may label your child as "bad" or "spoiled." Your child needs YOU to believe in their innate goodness. Remember, the biggest factor that determines whether a child succeeds or not is whether a caring adult believed in them and had a strong relationship with them.

You may be wondering what happened to Aidan.

That scene in church happened over ten years ago. After a thorough evaluation, Aidan was diagnosed to be in the autism spectrum. He underwent therapy and was also on medication for a while. Doing this broke the negative cycle and improved the relationships with people around him.

Today, he is a freshman at one of the country's top universities.

And – he even underwent training to become a server during mass! Looking at the teenager in the acolyte's uniform who obviously believes in his faith deeply and does his duties faithfully, you'd never guess he was that same boy who ran around the church like a wild animal.

Aidan's mom is glad that she never resorted to spanking, and instead got Aidan – and herself – the support he needs.

CHAPTER 10

CONCLUSION

Throughout this book, we've talked about Positive Parenting and why it works. We've gone on a journey to understand our kids' behavior. We've gone over several strategies to build a healthier relationship with our kids, help them learn the behaviors we expect from them, and guide them when they show disruptive behavior.

It may feel like a lot to do, but even just starting with one or two strategies can make a huge difference. That's why this book is here for you. Keep coming back to it to help you navigate future challenges. If you need more hands-on support, that's what our parent coaching programs are for.

There's no such thing as a perfect parent, and we don't aim for perfectly obedient and compliant kids either. Because in the end, what do we really want our kids to learn? What are our ultimate goals in parenting? What do we hope our children will become?

Do we want our children to simply obey orders without question? Is compliance our ultimate goal, or is there something more we're striving for?

In the 1960s, there was a series of famous experiments conducted by social psychologist Stanley Milgram. The experiment was designed to measure the willingness of participants to obey authority figures, even when it meant harming others.

Imagine that you were recruited for a study that you're told is a "learning experiment." Each time the "student" (who, without you knowing it, was part of the research team) made an error in recalling a word from a list, you're asked to deliver an "electric shock." This is actually a fake electric shock, but you don't know it's fake because the "student" screams and acts like they're in pain.

You hesitate, not wanting to hurt the "student," but someone who seems to be an authority figure tells you to give progressively stronger shocks – until you reach the zone marked "danger: severe shock." If just reading this makes you feel upset, you get an idea of just how disturbing these "obedience experiments" were.

So, what happened? 65% (!) – that's two-thirds – of the research participants listened to the "authority figure" and delivered to the maximum shock level! [53]

Why is it that a significant number of people are willing to administer what they believed were dangerous and even lethal electric shocks to a stranger, simply because an authority figure told them to do so?

Now, let's transpose this scenario onto our parenting. Do we want our children to blindly follow instructions, even if it leads to causing harm? Or do we wish to foster a sense of morality, critical thinking, and the courage to question authority when necessary?

We often hear adults complaining that "children today don't obey authority the way they used to." But isn't questioning and sometimes even refusing to obey a part of learning to think independently? Isn't this a sign that they are evaluating the instructions given to them before deciding on a course of action?

While no ethics board will ever approve a repeat of the Milgram experiments, a similar concept was replicated in some more recent studies that suggested the likelihood of blind obedience to authority has declined.[54]

---

[53] https://www.simplypsychology.org/milgram.html
[54] Twenge, J. M. (2009). Change over time in obedience: The jury's still out, but it might be decreasing. *American Psychologist*, 64(1), 28–31. Laurent Bègue & Kevin Vezirian (2023) The blind obedience of others: a better than average effect in a Milgram-like experiment, Ethics & Behavior, DOI: 10.1080/10508422.2023.2191322

Maybe today, more people will say, "I don't care who you are, but I'm not giving electric shocks to anyone! And what kind of crazy person would give electric shocks because someone failed to memorize a bunch of words?!" Isn't this the kind of courage and moral conviction we would want to instill in our children – over and above teaching compliance?

In our journey of parenting, let's aim to raise children who are not just obedient, but discerning. Let's strive to nurture kids who don't merely follow the rules, but who dare to stand up for what they believe is right. After all, it's these young minds that will shape the future of our society, and we owe it to them to provide a strong moral and ethical foundation to build upon.

In the end, we want to teach our kids a sense of right and wrong that becomes their internal compass even as they grow older. This is something we need to do as parents. We shouldn't abdicate this responsibility to other people, and definitely, this isn't something we leave them to figure out for themselves without any guidance from us!

Many parents today are afraid to take a stand on what they believe in because they're afraid of "brainwashing" their kids. Well, the reality is, our kids receive a lot of messages every day on what is "right" and "wrong," whether we like it or not.

If we don't take a stand and show our kids by example and let our kids know what we actually believe in, the only opinions kids will hear are the opinions of people on the internet or others who may not have our kids' best interests at heart. These will be the people "brainwashing" our kids!

In the end, it's about being a Discerning Parent. There's no one-size-fits-all and cookie-cutter approach to parenting. No single strategy will work for every child every time. And no single answer to questions like, "Should I insist on a rule, or should I give in?"

But you now have the science and the strategies. You know your child, your family, and your situation, and you also have your values, priorities, and intuition. With these, you can discern the best way to respond to the everyday parenting situations that will come your way.

BREAKING THE CYCLE

*M*any of the clients I work with are the "gamechangers" in their families. They may have been raised with fear, criticism, and harsh punishments and felt the trauma, and resolve not to raise their kids that way.

However, around them they hear people say, "It's impossible to raise a good child unless they're afraid of you." Or, "Positive parenting doesn't work. You really need to spank your kids."

We've already shared a lot of research evidence in this book. Now, I want to share a story to give further hope and inspiration to parents who may feel alone in wanting to move away from fear-based parenting and towards connection instead. Breaking the cycle can affect not just what happens today, but it will transform the lives of generations to come.

Dr. Isabel is a developmental and behavioral pediatrician, a colleague of mine I have known and worked with for over two decades. It has always amazed me how calm and resilient she is – and how she handles with grace challenges that often make others (including me!) want to give up.

She also introduced me to the idea of Positive Parenting when I was still a trainee in pediatrics, and I heard that her parents made it a point to practice Positive Parenting at a time when that term may not have been popular yet. It made me wonder if how she was raised was a huge factor in the extraordinary mental and emotional resilience she shows.

Sharing her story with you about how it is possible to break the cycle, and how this will create a huge transformation even decades from now, for future generations to come.

While this is Dr. Isabel's story I share, it is by no means unique. You may recognize how your own parents, in the best way they knew how, also tried to break negative parenting cycles, and we honor and appreciate them fully for doing so.

My parents did their best to show their human side to their children. I remember times when they apologized to me if they thought they failed or did something wrong. Although they were generally against spanking, I was spanked twice in my childhood. I don't remember being told it was because I was bad, but rather, my mother owned up to it, admitting that she had lost control.

My mother's voice, her way of speaking to me when I made mistakes, is the same way I speak to myself now. I think our parents' reactions to our mistakes shape the way we react to our own mistakes.

They would also share stories about their own upbringing, which was drastically different from the way they raised us. They were intentional about not repeating certain things they disagreed with from their upbringing while preserving the positive aspects.

One key lesson I learned from a parenting workshop was that parenting is not a natural process. A lot is learned, and much of it is based on our values and goals for our children and our families. We knew what values our parents considered important for our family.

They created a safe space for us, always encouraging kindness and respect. They were always supportive and understanding of our mistakes. They communicated with us extensively, through letters and personal talks, sharing specific compliments and recounting fond memories.

They chose to raise us differently from their own upbringing, breaking the cycle. This realization and decision was critical in becoming a better parent.

Parenting doesn't happen by chance but rather involves careful planning. My husband and I are intentional in planning how we raise our children, a decision inspired by my parents.

Being raised with the freedom to make mistakes allowed me to develop resilience and independence. This has been instrumental in my adult life, encouraging me to venture out of my comfort zone and try new things.

Now, as a parent myself, I understand the importance of providing a close-knit environment and understanding my children well. With the prevalence of technology, we face the challenge of maintaining internet safety, which requires constant monitoring and planning. Nonetheless, we strive to provide a balanced environment where we offer structure and guidance while still allowing our children to make choices.

ABOUT THE AUTHOR

Dr. Victoria Ang-Nolasco is a developmental and behavioral pediatrician, Positive Parenting coach and parent educator, and Mom. She is the host of the Discerning Parenting Podcast and author of *Toddler Talking: Boost Your Child's Language and Brain Development in Three Easy Steps*. She was also a clinical associate professor of pediatrics and university lecturer in brain psychology.

It's her mission to help parents find calm and joy in parenting through practical and science-backed strategies.

To learn more and access your Companion Guide and book bonuses, go to discerningparenting.com/behavior.

The QR Code below
will take you to the Amazon Sales Page.

www.ingramcontent.com/pod-product-compliance
Lightning Source LLC
Chambersburg PA
CBHW060610080526
44585CB00013B/761